MAYAN AND AZTEC MYTHOLOGY

Titles in the Mythology Series

American Indian Mythology
ISBN 0-7660-1411-8

Chinese Mythology
ISBN 0-7660-1412-6

Egyptian Mythology
ISBN 0-7660-1407-X

Gods and Goddesses in Greek Mythology
ISBN 0-7660-1408-8

Heroes in Greek Mythology
ISBN 0-7660-1560-2

Inuit Mythology
ISBN 0-7660-1559-9

Mayan and Aztec Mythology
ISBN 0-7660-1409-6

Roman Mythology
ISBN 0-7660-1558-0

~ MYTHOLOGY ~

MAYAN AND AZTEC MYTHOLOGY

Michael A. Schuman

Enslow Publishers, Inc.

40 Industrial Road	PO Box 38
Box 398	Aldershot
Berkeley Heights, NJ 07922	Hants GU12 6BP
USA	UK

http://www.enslow.com

Library of Congress Cataloging-in-Publication Data

Schuman, Michael.
    Mayan and Aztec mythology / Michael A. Schuman.
        p. cm. — (Mythology)
    Includes bibliographical references and index.
    Summary: Discusses various Mayan and Aztec myths, including creation stories and
    tales of principal gods and goddesses.
     ISBN 0-7660-1409-6
     1. Maya mythology. 2. Aztec mythology. 3. Maya gods—Juvenile literature. 4. Aztec
    gods—Juvenile literature. [1. Mayas—Folklore. 2. Aztecs—Folklore. 3. Indians of
    Mexico—Folklore. 4. Indians of Central America—Folklore. 5. Folklore—Mexico.
    6. Folklore—Central America.] I. Title. II. Mythology (Berkeley Heights, N.J.)
    F1434.2.R3 S38   2000
    299'.72—dc21   00-028779

Printed in the United States of America

10 9 8 7 6 5

To Our Readers: We have done our best to make sure all Internet addresses in this book were active and appropriate when we went to press. However, the author and the publisher have no control over and assume no liability for the material available on those Internet sites or on other Web sites they may link to. Any comments or suggestions can be sent by e-mail to comments@enslow.com or to the address on the back cover.

Cover and Illustrations by William Sauts Bock

◁◁ CONTENTS ◁◁

AZTEC JAGUAR SCULPTURE

VOLCANO POPOCATEPETL

EL TAJIN

TULA

TEOTIHUACAN
TLATILCO

VERACRUZ
CACAXTLA

SAN LORENZ

TENOCHTITLAN
(MEXICO CITY)

CHOLULA
PUEBLA

SCULPTURE OF
QUETZALCOATL

AZTECS

AZTEC
GRAIN BIN

Pacific Ocean

OAXACA

AZTEC
RAIN
GOD HOLDING
MAIZE

Pacific

CEREMONIAL CENTER

MAP of MAYAS
and AZTECS

SCULPTURE OF AZTEC CITIZEN

MAYA MOON GODDESS

MAYA PALACE

MAYA CEREMONIAL CENTER

G   of   Mexico

YUCATAN

CHICHEN ITZE

UXMAL
JAINA

TULUM

LOWLAND MAYA

MAYA
STONE
JAGUAR
THRONE

LA VENTA
PALENQUE

ALTUN HA
LAMANAI

UAXACTUN

CHIAPA DE CORZO

TIKAL

MAYA DEATH GOD

HIGHLAND

MAYA MERCHANT

IZAPA

OCOS

MAYA

N
W   E
S

▷◁ PREFACE ▷◁

ALL ABOUT THE MAYAS AND AZTECS

Many people associate mythology only with the Greeks and Romans. After all, those two civilizations have supplied the most famous myths and gods in history. However, it is important to realize that all cultures in all sections of the world have their own unique mythologies. That is certainly true for the sophisticated Mayan and Aztec civilizations that developed in Mesoamerica.

Mesoamerica is a geographical area that covers most of what is now Mexico, Guatemala, Belize, and other parts of Central America. Even though the early Mesoamerican cultures from which the Mayas and Aztecs emerged were different in many ways, they encountered one another often because of trade, migration, and conquest. As a result, they share some of the same characteristics, and their religions and myths share some of the same themes.

For example, most Mesoamerican cultures were very interested in keeping track of time, so they developed complicated calendars which they used to predict important events, such as the changing of the seasons and eclipses of the sun or moon. They believed that they needed to know when these events would happen so they could make offerings and sacrifices to the gods, the forces of good and evil who controlled their lives.

The great civilizations that emerged from the early Mesoamerican cultures shared many other characteristics as well. Their religious practices included human sacrifice, which they believed was necessary to provide the blood and human hearts that nourished the gods. They developed hieroglyphic writing, which was based on pictures. One of the ways we know how they lived and thought is through the hieroglyphics they carved in stone or wrote in books called codices, which were made of fig-bark paper or deerskin that was folded like screens.

Both the Mayas and the Aztecs developed complex systems of government, constructed great cities that included temples and monuments, used sophisticated agricultural methods, and held large markets at which all kinds of food and goods were sold. Their societies included different classes, or groups, of people. The people at the top, such as the nobility, had the greatest wealth, while most ordinary people, such as peasants and laborers, were very poor. Mesoamerican societies also included warriors, priests, skilled artisans (such as carpenters), merchants, architects, astronomers, and artists. There were also professional dancers, singers, and musicians, who often participated in the many religious celebrations.

Among the most interesting features that archeologists discovered when they began excavating ancient Meso-american cities were ball courts made of stone. These courts were used for playing a very rough game in which two teams of men would try to pass a heavy rubber ball through a ring. The men had to keep the ball in motion by hitting it with their hips, shoulders, or other part of their torso, and perhaps their head. They could not use their hands or feet. From what we know, this game was very violent and often part of a religious ritual. Players were often injured, and sometimes the men on the losing team became sacrificial victims. As you will see, ball games were so important that they appear in Mesoamerican mythology.

Mesoamerican civilizations thrived until the arrival of the Spanish in the 1500s. The Spanish *conquistadores*

(conquerors) and the Catholic priests who accompanied or followed them brought enormous changes, most of them destructive. The epidemic diseases they carried, such as smallpox, influenza, and measles, were deadly to the native populations. They concentrated the people into Spanish-style villages and towns so they would be easier to control. Despite the complexity and sophistication of the Mayan and Aztec civilizations they discovered, the Spanish felt that their religion, Christianity, made them morally superior. They believed that their Christian beliefs were better than the native Americans' religious teachings. In the name of religion, the invaders destroyed many buildings, books, and works of art.

But the Spanish also helped to preserve information about Mesoamerican civilizations, religions, and mythology. Their letters, books, and documents tell us about the cultures they discovered. More importantly, they taught nobles and others in the civilizations they conquered to use the Roman alphabet to write their own history and mythology in their own language.

The Mayas

While the Aztec civilization developed in the part of Mexico that is now Mexico City, the Mayan civilization developed farther south, in what is now northern Guatemala and Belize. Today, there are about six million Mayas, mostly in Guatemala, where Mayas are about half of the population.

The Mayas have a longer history than the Aztecs. Researchers believe that by 1800 B.C.–1500 B.C., the earliest Mayas were cultivating maize (corn), beans, and squash, and had begun constructing permanent villages. These villages consisted mostly of one-room houses made of mud, with thatched roofs, but they also included structures that were designed for ceremonial purposes.

Mayan culture and civilization reached its peak during the Classic Period, from 300 A.D.–900 A.D. During that period, the Mayas built great cities with pyramids, temples, monuments, palaces, and ball courts. Yet in a single century, from 800 A.D. to 900 A.D., Mayan civilization declined, for reasons no one has been able to learn. The Mayas abandoned one city after another, sometimes so quickly that buildings and monuments were left partly constructed. Over the centuries, the jungle reclaimed the temples, courtyards, and palaces, transforming them into ruins to be discovered by archeologists in our own time.

The Mayas did not disappear, however. Many of them moved north into the Yucatan Peninsula, part of what is now Mexico. One of the groups that remained in what is now Guatemala became known as the Quiche (kee-CHAY) Maya, one of perhaps a dozen major Mayan tribes who lived well until they were conquered by the Spanish.

Thanks to the Mayas' ability to leave a written record, they have provided one of the most detailed mythologies of any group. Archaeologists have found written accounts of their history, rituals, and myths in hieroglyphics carved into stone pillars, doorways, and stairways. Four original Mayan codices survive, although one is little more than a fragment. The most complete codex is now in Dresden, Germany. The others in are in Paris, France; Madrid, Spain; and New York City. The original manuscript of their great epic, the Popol Vuh (POH-pole VOO), has never been found, but educated Mayans transcribed it into the Quiche language in the 1550s.

The Mayas had two ways of figuring time. Their sacred calendar, for reasons no one knows, calculated a year of 260 days. This calendar was used for religious purposes.

For example, the day on which a baby was born according to the sacred calendar determined which god would be that child's patron saint.

The Mayas also had a civil calendar that was similar to our own. This calendar, which was used for everyday purposes, was based on a solar year of 360 ordinary days, plus five unlucky days at the end.

In addition to their other accomplishments, the Mayas seriously studied the planets and stars. In fact, they were so knowledgeable in the field of astronomy that they could accurately predict eclipses of the sun and moon. Centuries before the invention of modern astronomical tools, the Mayas had already charted the courses of Mercury, Venus, and Mars.

Not only were the Mayas sophisticated astronomers, but they also developed a system for mathematics that included the concept of zero. The use of the zero, which is needed for making any complex calculations, was developed in only two Old World cultures—by the Hindus and the Babylonians.

The ingenious Mayan people built great cities hacked out of the wild jungle, without the benefit of motorized construction vehicles. Mayan engineers constructed causeways and elevated walkways from stone. They crafted immense pyramids, some of which were two hundred feet high, from stone, earth, and rubble. These pyramids dominated the great Mayan cities, which had names like Chichen Itze (chee-CHEN eet-SAH), Tikal (tee-KAL), Uxmal (oosh-MAHL), and Palenque (pah-LENK-ay).

These commanding pyramids were the central points of wide, open plazas, and they were usually surrounded by temples, ball courts, and other buildings. The courts were the settings for the ball game the Mayas called *pohatok* (POHK-uh-tohk), which played such a vital role in Mayan life that it figured in their myths. Ruins of Mayan cities in places such as the Yucatan peninsula of Mexico, Belize, Guatemala, and Honduras are visited every year by thousands of people ranging from casual tourists to professional archaeologists and anthropologists.

The pyramids were religious structures, the Mayan equivalent of churches, synagogues, and mosques. Members of the nobility were buried in them, and human sacrifices of both Mayan nobles and prisoners of war took place on top of them. To us the idea of human sacrifice may sound gruesome or primitive, but to the Mayas it was the best way to please the gods. These gods, the Mayas believed strongly, controlled both the heavens and the activities of the people on Earth. They believed that if they did not perform these ritual sacrifices, there would be chaos in the world.

Although the Mayas sometimes sacrificed animals, the supreme sacrifice was human life. Some Mayan victims, including prisoners of war, had their heads sliced off. Others had their hearts cut out while they were still alive. Still others had parts of their bodies mutilated so they would bleed abundantly. This blood was then dropped on paper made of tree bark and burned. The smoke from the blood was believed to carry messages to important Mayan gods, including Itzamna (its-ahm-NAH) and Ix Chel (ISH chel), the mother and father of all other gods.

In addition to their accomplishments in architecture and astronomy, the Mayas had superior knowledge of farming. To a great extent, they lived on a diet of maize. Mayan farmers grew maize in small garden plots called *milpas* (MIHL-pahs), which they cultivated in the middle of raw jungle terrain. But the Mayas did not live on maize alone. They also grew chili peppers, squash, and beans for food, as well as cotton for fabric.

The Mayas were smart enough to know not to overwork the soil, a mistake many settlers of European backgrounds and their descendants made years later when they settled the New World. Mayan workers purposely stopped farming each milpa after working it for only a few years. This conservation method prevented the soil from being overworked, which would have made it barren and useless for the future cultivation of plants.

By the time the Spanish *conquistadores* invaded the Mayan lands in the 1500s, most of the Mayas had moved to the Yucatan Peninsula in Southeastern Mexico. What the Spanish found was the remains of a civilization that reached its greatest heights several centuries earlier. Yet the civilization they found was still for the most part larger, cleaner, and more efficiently run than the cities they had left behind in Spain.

The Spanish did not have an easy time conquering the Mayas. Over the course of 180 years, the Mayas defeated three Spanish armies. But the last Mayan city fell to the Spanish in 1697, although some small, isolated villages avoided surrender to the Spanish for years afterward.

The Aztecs

The Aztecs, who developed a great but short-lived civilization in central Mexico, are descended from a warlike tribe known as the Toltecs. In the tenth century A.D., the Toltecs built a great city called Tula to the north of what is now Mexico City. But only two and a half centuries later, in the middle of the 12th century, the Toltecs were conquered by a nomadic tribe called the Chichimeca. The Toltecs dispersed in all directions, leaving a legacy of legends and religious traditions that would become important elements of Aztec culture.

According to the Aztecs, their original homeland was an island in a lake called Aztlan, which means "White Land." Researchers are not exactly sure where Aztlan was, or even whether it actually existed. The word may simply refer to a general area northwest of present-day Mexico City. It may have been as close as sixty miles to Mexico City, or it may have been as distant from Mexico City as the states of Arizona and New Mexico.[1]

By the time the Spanish arrived in the 1500s, the Aztecs had become rulers of a vast empire. However, that empire began humbly, when a small wandering tribe took refuge from hostile neighbors on a swampy island near the western shore of Lake Texcoco in the Valley of Mexico.

In 1325 A.D., the Aztecs founded the city of Tenochtitlan (tay-NOTCH-tee-TLAHN) on this island in the middle of the lake, not far from the current site of Mexico City. Legends say that their tribal war god and symbol of the sun, Huitzilopochtli (Wee-tsee-loh-POHCH-tlee), had led them to the island, where they saw an eagle with a serpent in its beak. The eagle told them to build temples in this place and nourish the sun with the sacrifice of humans. The picture of the eagle with the serpent in its beak is shown on the Mexican flag today.

Tenochtitlan, which translates as "place of the stone cactus," became the Aztec capital, and by the 1400s, it had become a grand, thriving city, thanks to its people's advanced engineering projects and great military strength. Like the Mayas, the Aztecs used their intelligence and skill to build causeways and roadways. They found it necessary to construct causeways to connect their island city to the mainland. In addition, they dug canals and aqueducts to transport freight and people. To secure their place in the region and expand their empire, Aztec rulers waged war and created alliances with other tribes in the region.

Like the Mayas, the Aztecs built religious temples in the form of pyramids throughout their capital. The most notable was the Great Temple, a huge structure embellished with twin stone staircases side by side. On top of the Great Temple were shrines to two powerful gods: Huitzilopochtli, and Tlaloc (TLAH-lohk), the god of rain. It was at the shrine to Tlaloc that human sacrifices were made. Smaller temples discovered near the Great Temple included one with a platform made up of more than 200 skulls. Experts believe that the heads were those of sacrificial victims.

Two other very important Aztec gods were Quetzalcoatl (ket-SAHL-koh-AHTL) and Tezcatlipoca (tes-CAHT-li-PO-kah). Quetzalcoatl, whose name means "feathered serpent," was viewed as the god of wind and life. Tezcatlipoca, or "smoking mirror," was identified as the god of night and sorcery. The Aztec kings claimed that they were Tezcatlipoca's representatives on Earth.

Aztec society was divided into three main classes: nobles, commoners, and slaves. For the most part, the nobility was made up of people who had been born into this class, priests, and those who had earned their noble rank, such as military leaders. As in all societies, people in the higher classes had the most wealth and enjoyed special privileges.

Some commoners were permitted to own land on which they could build a home. However, other commoners were very poor laborers or tenant farmers who worked for other people and could live on their land only by permission. Sometimes the male children of commoners were allowed to attend special schools where they studied the arts of war and religion.

Slaves were similar to indentured servants. Many were poor people who had sold themselves into slavery to pay off their debts, and others were people who had been captured in war. Creative, clever slaves could escape from a life sentence of hard toil. Those who ran away from their owners and managed to reach the royal palace safely were awarded their freedom. The children of slaves were free, and most slaves could win or buy their freedom.

To feed themselves, the Aztecs built floating gardens called *chinampas* (chee-NAHM-pahs) which were among the most fertile agricultural lands in the New World. The *chinampas* did not really float. Made of layers of silt and reeds, they were held in place by tree roots. On the *chinampas*, Aztec farmers grew squash, corn, grains, and beans, and for religious ceremonies, flowers. They used canoes to carry produce from the gardens to markets in the city. Some *chinampas* still exist today at Xochimilico and Mixquic.

The Aztec diet included animals and plants many people in the United States today would consider disgusting, such as locusts, algae, larvae nests, and iguanas. They also dined on foods commonly eaten in Mexico and elsewhere today, such as maize, sweet potatoes, and tomatoes. As it was for the Mayas, maize was the Aztecs' staple food. They ate it in porridge, tortillas, and pancakes, which they often stuffed with treats such as cactus worms and tadpoles. The Aztec diet also included meat from the bountiful animals in their region, such as ducks and deer.

The Aztecs loved eating big meals, especially during religious ceremonies, which were often a mixture of joyfulness and solemnity. These ceremonies usually included a religious ritual, followed by dancing and a large feast. One of the biggest rituals was called *hueytecuilhuitl*, which means "great feast of the lords." For a period of ten days, celebrations began each evening and lasted all night long. The ritual concluded with the beheading of a young woman who was sacrificed as a symbol of the goddess of the young corn. Aztec religious rituals sometimes included a ball game called *tlachtli* (T'LAHCH-tlee) which was similar to the Mayans' game of *pohatok*.

The Aztecs' civilization thrived well into the 1400s, when they formed a triple alliance with two other native peoples, the Texcoco and Tlacopan (T'LAH-coh-pan). In turn, the triple alliance conquered two other native peoples in 1487, and remained a major force in the region for more than 30 years. The beginning of the end came in 1519, when the first Europeans came from Spain under the leadership of conquistador Hernando Cortez. The Aztec ruler, Montezuma II, tried to convince Cortez not to enter Tenochtitlan. However, Montezuma's pleas were ignored by Cortez, who invaded the Aztec capital.

In fact, many Aztecs welcomed Cortez, whom they thought to be the god Quetzalcoatl because the feathered serpent god had always been assumed to have fair skin and a beard. Cortez and his army took advantage of this supposed resemblance to the Aztecs' important god, helping themselves to the Aztecs' gold and other material riches.

In spite of his welcome, Cortez feared Montezuma and thought the ruler might turn on him. So Cortez made a logical military move. He captured Montezuma and held him hostage. In 1520, a group of Aztecs rebelled against Cortez and his Spanish army. In the revolt, Montezuma was killed, and Cortez and his men were forced out of Tenochtitlan. The next year, Cortez returned, and after a three-month-long siege of Tenochtitlan, the Aztec capital fell to the Spanish. The date was August 13, 1521. The Aztec empire had been destroyed.

Myths and Lifestyles

As you read the myths in this book, you will note that many of the Mayan and Aztec gods relate strongly to the lifestyles of the people. Since both peoples relied heavily on farming for survival, they believed in gods who ruled over the elements like rain, or over crops such as maize. These were warlike cultures, so there were warrior gods to guide them in battle and give them courage. And because they shared the same basic life cycles of people everywhere, they believed in gods of childbirth and the underworld, as well.

You will also discover there are many similarities between Mayan and Aztec myths. Does that suggest the two groups descended from the same people? Peter Vanderloo, a professor at Northern Arizona University and expert on the Mayan and Aztec cultures, admits that it is difficult to say if the Aztecs and Mayas descended from the same ancestors. If they do, it appears that the common ancestor goes back many centuries. Perhaps the common traits of the Mayas and Aztecs evolved because they shared the same part of the world, saw the same animals around them, and ate the same food to stay alive.

1

THE CREATION OF PEOPLE ACCORDING TO THE POPOL VUH

INTRODUCTION

Holy writings are one element that many religions have in common. These texts often describe everything about a particular culture, from its religious laws to how it views the creation of the universe. The religious texts of Jews and Christians are called the Bible; for Muslims, the religious text is the Koran. For the Quiche Maya, the most important religious text was their sacred epic, the Popol Vuh.

The original manuscript of the Popol Vuh, which some researchers call the "Council Book"[1] and others call "the Book of the Community," has never been found. But in the middle of the 16th Century, a Quiche Maya used Roman characters to write it out in his own language, and in the early 1700s, a Dominican priest named Francisco Ximeinez copied it. It has been studied many times over by historians, experts on religion, and philosophers.

In addition to legends and myths that had been handed down for generations, the Popol Vuh is filled with scientific data, especially details regarding the stars and planets. Like a modern almanac, it included facts, such as the rising and setting dates of certain planets, but it also contained information about and pictures of each planet's attending gods. Mayan rulers seriously considered all aspects of this information when deciding on the proper time to hold a ceremony, begin a battle, or prepare for war or famine.

Like the Bible, the Popol Vuh was told in different versions. And like the Bible, the Popol Vuh's versions were fairly similar to one another. In one version of the Popol Vuh, its writers explained why Mayan rulers found these writings so important.

"They knew whether war would occur; everything they saw was clear to them. Whether there would be death, or whether there would be famine, or whether quarrels would occur, they knew it for certain, since there was a place to see it, there was a book. 'Council Book' was their name for it."[2]

The mythologies of all cultures are based on stories about the world's most fascinating mystery: How the universe and its human population were created. The following myth explains how creation took place, according to the Quiche Maya holy book, the Popol Vuh.

THE CREATION OF PEOPLE ACCORDING TO THE POPOL VUH

Δ'Δ'Δ'Δ'Δ'Δ'Δ'Δ'Δ'Δ'Δ'Δ'Δ'Δ'Δ'Δ'Δ'Δ'Δ'Δ'Δ'Δ'Δ'Δ'Δ'Δ'Δ'Δ'Δ

Before human beings, animals, grass, trees, and rocks were created, there was nothing but sky above and ocean below. There was not even any light or sound. There were, however, gods, called Creators, who lived hidden under layers of green and blue feathers deep in the ocean.

The Creators were tired of living in the bleak darkness under so many layers, so one day they got together and planned to fill the vast voids of the cosmos. They called out, "Let creation begin! Let the void be filled! Let the sea recede, revealing the surface of the Earth! Earth, arise! Let it be done!" [3]

And so the Earth, with its hills and streams and lakes and trees, rose up from the sea. At first, the Creators were thrilled with their rolling hills, rushing streams, and handsome cypress trees. However, although the new world was beautiful, it was also painfully quiet. So the Creators used their skills to make animals, such as deer and birds.

Then the gods commanded, "You, the deer: Sleep along the rivers, in the canyons. Be here in the meadows, in the thickets, in the forests. Multiply yourselves. You will stand and walk on all fours.

"You, precious birds: Your nests, your houses are in the

trees, in the bushes. Multiply there, scatter there, in the branches of trees, the branches of bushes."[4]

The Creators were very pleased with the animals, but there was still a problem. The gods wanted to be praised for their excellent efforts and adored by their creations. Animals could squawk and squeal and make other illiterate sounds, but they could not do verbal justice in praising their makers. The Creators became disheartened with the limitations of their work. So they ordered, "We will not take from you that which we have given you. However, because you cannot praise us and love us, we will make other beings who will. These new creatures will be superior to you and will rule you. It is your destiny that they will tear apart and eat your flesh. Let it be done!"[5]

The Creators then tried to create a class of creatures superior to animals. These creatures, the Maya people, would be able to speak words. But it was not an easy job to carry out.

First, the Creators used mud to make the people. Yet the mud people were not the kind of beings the Creators had in mind. They were soft and limp, and had trouble standing upright. Even worse, after it rained, they became wet and soggy and could not stand up at all. In addition, they were unable to see and had no brains. They could speak, but without a brain to guide their thinking, the people's sounds were gibberish. Without wasting any more time, the Creators destroyed these mud people soon after they had been made.

The Creators tried again. This time they used wood to make human beings. The stick people were an improvement over the mud people. The sturdy wood allowed them to stand up and walk. Like the mud people, the wood people were able to speak. And so they lived and multiplied.

Yet soon the Creators realized that, like the mud people, the wood people had no minds, so their words made no sense. They did not have blood flowing through their bodies, so their skin was dry and crusty rather than fresh and firm. They had no hearts, so their faces had no expressions. Even more important, they had no souls, so they did not know the difference between right and wrong. These ignorant beings burned the bottoms of their cooking pots and tortilla griddles, and beat and starved their dogs. Finally, the Creators realized they would have to destroy the stick people and try a third time to create creatures who were more complete.

In destroying the stick people, the gods humiliated them. First the Creators unleashed a flood of a sticky sap-like substance. The wooden humans tried to escape, but their dogs, their former victims, would not let them do so. The dogs the wooden people had once beaten and starved so savagely now gained revenge by using their sharp teeth to bite the people and slash their faces. The griddles and pots the people had once burned so thoughtlessly also retaliated by burning the people back.

A few stick people managed to break free from the attackers they had once mistreated and tried to escape the flood of sticky sap. They climbed trees and hid on the roofs

of houses. Yet even the trees and houses demanded vengeance. The trees shook their branches until the people fell to the ground. The houses collapsed rather than protect these wooden humans. And when the wooden race of people tried to hide inside caves, the caves closed up. Most of the people drowned in the sap. The few who did survive had their faces twisted until they no longer resembled humans. They became a new kind of animal, called monkeys.

For a third time, the Creators met to put their heads together. They needed a new way to bring to life the race of humans they had envisioned. Just as the Creators' meeting began, four animals came to visit: a mountain cat, a coyote, a crow, and a parrot. The animals told the Creators about an amazing food called maize, or corn, that grew nearby in an area called Broken Place. The Creators were very curious about this new food and wished to see it for themselves. So the animal quartet led the Creators to Broken Place where they found corn growing in abundance. The Creators realized at once that this was the key ingredient that had been missing. It was exactly what they needed to make the kind of creatures they had hoped to place on Earth.

The Creators got busy right away. They mashed corn into meal and used it to make four strong, handsome men who became known as the Four Fathers. Then they ground more corn into a liquid. The Creators offered the new potion to the men they had just made. The men drank it, and suddenly they had muscles and energy. While the men slept, the Creators made each one a wife as beautiful as the men were handsome.

The Four Fathers gratefully thanked the Creators for bringing them into the world, and for having been given an intelligence so superior that they were aware of all knowledge in the world. Much of their intelligence was aided by the men's powerful eyesight. The Four Fathers told their Creators, "We can see, we can hear, we can move and think and speak. We feel and know everything; we can see everything in the Earth and in the sky. Thank you for having made us . . ."[6]

That suddenly led to a new problem. As they watched this new race of people, the Creators realized that by the making humans too perfect, they had made a mistake. If these people continued to see and know everything, then they would not be human beings but gods, just like themselves. It was clear that the Creators would have to do something to limit the intelligence and power of their handiwork.

So the Creators blew a mist into the Four Fathers' eyes. The mist had the same effect on the eyes of the men as a person's breath does on a mirror. The men could still see, but not as far. They could still think, but now their all-knowing intelligence was reduced to a more modest range of knowledge.

Soon the Four Fathers and their wives had children. Then their children had children, and before long there were many human beings on the Earth.

QUESTIONS AND ANSWERS

Q: *What fault did the Creators find with the animals they had made?*

A: The Creators wanted to be praised and loved by their creations, but the animals could not speak.

Q: *What were some of the problems with the mud people made by the Creators?*

A: When dry, they had trouble standing upright. When wet, they could not stand at all. They also had no brains and could not think or speak a language.

Q: *What was the biggest problem with the wood people?*

A: They had no hearts and no souls, and they did not know right from wrong.

Q: *How were monkeys created?*

A: Monkeys were made from the few wood people who were able to escape the great flood of sticky sap.

Q: *Who came to the Creators' third meeting and what did they tell the Creators?*

A: A mountain cat, a coyote, a crow, and a parrot came to tell the Creators of an amazing food called maize, which grew in an area called Broken Place.

Q: *How were the Four Fathers made?*

A: The Creators mashed corn into meal to make the Four Fathers' bodies. Then the Creators ground more corn into a liquid. When the Four Fathers drank it, they suddenly had muscles and energy.

Q: *Why were the Creators unhappy with the first intelligent humans they made?*

A: With their powerful intelligence and eyesight, the humans were able to know too much. They might challenge their Creators with these godlike powers and knowledge.

Q: *How did the Creators limit the powers and knowledge of the humans?*

A: They blew a mist into the Four Fathers' eyes.

EXPERT COMMENTARY

Roberta H. and Peter T. Markman are professors in southern California and authors of books about Latin American mythology. In *The Flayed God: The Mythology of Mesoamerica*, the Markmans explain the importance of impairing the vision of the newly created Mayan people. They liken this tale to the Greek myth of Oedipus (ED-uh-puhs).

Oedipus was the son of the king and queen of Thebes. As a baby, he was abandoned and left for dead by his father, but was rescued and grew to adulthood. As an adult, he met his natural father whom he mistook for a robber and murdered. He then married his mother, not knowing who she was. Later, after realizing what she and Oedipus had done, his mother killed herself, and Oedipus cut out his eyes.

"Like the Greek hero Oedipus, man would live with only limited vision and 'could only see [what was] nearby.'"[7] According to the Markmans, being limited to seeing what is "nearby" is a metaphor, or a comparison, to having their view "of the hidden world of the spirit," [or the workings of their gods] also limited at the same time.[8]

Scholar Ralph Nelson, who published a translation of the Popol Vuh in 1976, wrote in his introduction to that book that the Mayas' idea of nature may have influenced this story of creation.

Nature also suggests a unity, and the idea may have existed, too, that all elements of life are an intricate part of the whole. The bug on the leaf and the passing cloud are brothers, in this sense, part of the absolute entity. This view is close to the pantheistic view that the world *is* god. The multiplicity of later religions would suggest that this is an early view, and it is well illustrated in the story of the stick men in the Popol Vuh. The stick men, after falling out of divine favor, find out too late that all things (whether stone . . . or the cooking pot) lead lives similar to their own, lives that they had been abusing.[9]

2

SEVEN MACAW AND HIS SONS

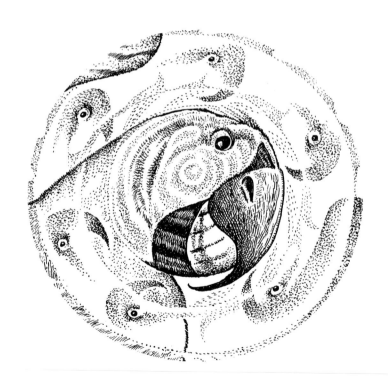

INTRODUCTION

The first major portion of the Popol Vuh deals with the creation story. Part of this story concerns the heroic deeds of two sets of twins. One set of twins, about whom you will learn in the next chapter, was lured to the Underworld where they were murdered. Those twins were the father and uncle of the twins you will learn about in this chapter: Hunahpu (hoo-nah-POOH) and Xbalanque (sh-bah-LAHN-kay), who came to be known among the Mayas as the Hero Twins.

Twins are often found in Mesoamerican creation myths. The Mesoamerican cultures feared twins because they considered them abnormal. They believed that twins had religious significance, and that they foreshadowed important events. They are often portrayed as monster-killers and heroes who create order, but they also represent conflict and change.

The tales about the Hero Twins take place in the middle of the creation story of the Popol Vuh, after the stick people are destroyed but before the gods meet with the four animals who suggest making people from corn. This tale only makes sense if the proper time frame is kept in mind. And despite the fact that the Hero Twins' adventures occur in the middle of the creation myth, experts consider the following story to be a separate myth in its own right.

In the Popol Vuh, the Hero Twins go down to the underworld to avenge the murder of their father and uncle. But first, they challenge a conceited bird named Seven Macaw, who claims to be the sun. A macaw is a large, showy type of parrot with a curved bill and long tail that is found throughout Central America. The macaw's feathers are a rainbow of vivid colors.

The twins know that Seven Macaw is not the sun, and they think it is their destiny to fight and destroy this bird so that the real sun can take its rightful place in the sky. They also take on Seven Macaw's two sons, who cause their own kind of trouble.

SEVEN MACAW AND HIS SONS

Between the time that the earth had emerged from the sea and the sun had risen in the sky, there lived a macaw whose name was Itzam-Yeh (its-am-YEH), translated as Seven Macaw. Seven Macaw had a very high opinion of himself. Because his eyes were gemstones and his teeth shone like the Sun itself, he was convinced that, in fact, he was the sun. He was so self-absorbed that he announced that some day he would be the moon, as well.

The Hero Twins, Hunahpu and Xbalanque, felt that Seven Macaw was too boastful and was giving false impressions to the people. Clearly, he was not the sun. The twins decided he needed to be punished.

So the twins made plans to shoot Seven Macaw when they could distract the colorful bird. Finally, they found the perfect time to do so. Seven Macaw was eating lunch in a nance tree. (The nance tree still grows in the wilds of present-day Yucatan and is known for producing a luscious fruit.)

Hunahpu used a hollow pipe called a blowgun to shoot Seven Macaw with a pellet. The gun's pellet tore through the bird's mouth, breaking his jaw and injuring his precious eyes. The jewels in his mouth and eyes were severely damaged. The impact of the shot forced Seven Macaw to fall from the nance tree. However, Seven Macaw

was still dangerous. When Hunahpu approached Seven Macaw, the boastful bird bit off the twin's arm and escaped with it. When he returned to his home, Seven Macaw hung the arm over a fire.

Hunahpu and his brother tried hard to think of a way to get the arm back. Finally, after meeting with an elderly man and woman who were wrinkled, gray, and walked crookedly, the twins came up with a plan. The old couple agreed to pretend they were the twins' grandparents, and the foursome set out to find Seven Macaw. When they arrived at Seven Macaw's house, the old man told the bird that the twins were their grandsons. The old man added that he was an expert in fixing broken jaws and curing damaged eyes. As the twins had hoped, Seven Macaw then asked the grandfather to help him restore his damaged jeweled features.

First, the old man pulled the gemstones out of Seven Macaw's mouth and eyes and replaced them with kernels of white corn. When the old man was finished and the shiny jewels had been removed from the bird's face, Seven Macaw could no longer claim he looked like the sun. Now, he just looked like an average bird. Robbed of his source of conceit and vanity, Seven Macaw no longer had any reason to live, and he keeled over and died. As soon as he was dead, Hunahpu retrieved his arm from above the fireplace and placed it back on his body. It reattached itself perfectly.

Seven Macaw was survived by two sons. One was named Zipacna (zip-ak-NAH), or Alligator. The other was called Two-his-leg, and also called Earthquake. Like his father, Alligator also made boastful claims. He bragged that he was the maker of the mountains.

One day Alligator was resting by the water's edge when he saw a group of four hundred sons carrying a tree

to use as a post for a house they were building. Alligator asked the boys if he could help them. They gladly accepted his offer, and they let Alligator haul the tree to the door of the four hundred boys' house. The boys were impressed by Alligator's strength, but they also felt threatened by it, and believed Alligator might use his strength to hurt them. This strong beast must be killed, they thought.

The four hundred boys put their heads together and came up with what they considered a foolproof way to lead Alligator to his death. First, they would ask Alligator to do them a favor and dig a deep hole in the earth. When it was done, they would ask Alligator to crawl inside it. Then the boys would throw a wooden beam into the hole. They expected the weight of the beam to land on their trapped victim and crush him to death.

But Alligator was smart. He knew the boys wanted to kill him. So while he was digging the hole, he also unearthed an escape tunnel to a side of the hole. Alligator climbed into the hole, then tucked himself in the safety tunnel. He called out to the boys, announcing in a loud voice that their hole was complete. The boys then dropped the beam in the hole, unaware that Alligator sat safely to one side.

Convinced that Alligator was dead, the four hundred sons held a celebration. They partied so hard and drank so much that they became intoxicated. In fact, they were so drunk that they never even noticed when Alligator crawled out of his safety tunnel. Alligator picked up the boys' house and toppled it on their heads. All of the four hundred boys died under the weight of their home, and it was said that they became the stars in the sky.

The Hero Twins, Hunahpu and Xbalanque, were saddened by the death of the four hundred sons. They considered Alligator as treacherous as the boys had. So the twins planned to kill Alligator just as they had killed his father, Seven Macaw.

The twins planned to catch Alligator by offering him his favorite food, crabs. They crafted a magnificent artificial crab made from prairie grass, bamboo, and stone. Then they placed it in a canyon at the base of a mountain called Meavan (mee-VAN).

The twins found Alligator in the water and asked him what he was doing. Just as they had hoped, Alligator replied that he was looking for food. He said that he could not find any crabs or fish, and had not eaten for two days. Excitedly, the twins told Alligator about the gigantic crab they said they had just seen in the canyon at the foot of Meavan. Alligator drooled at the thought of such a treat and begged the twins to take him to it. So the three journeyed to Meavan with Alligator growing more excited with each step. However, just as he entered the canyon and spied the massive crab, the big mountain collapsed on Alligator's chest. Alligator could not move and turned to stone.

As it turned out, Seven Macaw's other son, Two-his-leg, was no less boastful than his father and brother, Alligator. Two-his-leg strongly stated that he was the destroyer of mountains. All he had to do, he bragged, was stamp his feet to make mountains tumble. One day, Hunahpu and Xbalanque confronted Two-his-leg and told him that recently they had discovered the highest mountain they had ever seen in their lives. They asked Two-his-leg if he thought he could knock down even this mammoth mountain.

With his usual vanity, Two-his-leg assured the twins that he could. To prove his boast, he asked the twins to take him to this mountain. On their way to the mountain, the Hero Twins became hungry. As was their custom, they pulled out their blowguns and killed a few birds, which they then roasted for dinner. Two-his-leg had no idea that the bird dinner was part of a plan to kill him.

The twins took one bird and cooked it together with a heavy chunk of the earth. Graciously, they invited Two-his-leg to join them for a delicious feast. They offered Two-his-leg a slice of the earth-laden bird, and he ate it and the piece of earth enthusiastically. When they finished their feast, all three got up and walked toward the enormous mountain.

But the weight of the meal he had just eaten made Two-his-leg feel incredibly weak. Suddenly, he could hardly stand on his legs. In that condition, he definitely could not make a mountain crash to the ground. The Hero Twins tied Two-his-leg up with ease, knocked him down, and killed him. Two-his-leg, otherwise known as Earthquake, has been permanently buried in the ground ever since. And ever after, whenever he moves in his grave, he shakes the world.

QUESTIONS AND ANSWERS

Q: *Why did Seven Macaw believe he was the sun?*

A: His eyes and teeth, made of precious jewels, shone with the power of the sun.

Q: *What caused the death of Seven Macaw?*

A: An elderly man replaced the gemstones from Seven Macaw's mouth and eyes with white corn. Seven Macaw no longer had self-esteem, and since he no longer felt superior, he felt he had no reason to live.

Q: *How did Alligator kill the four hundred sons?*

A: The four hundred sons were so intoxicated after celebrating that they did not see that Alligator was preparing to pull their house down on their heads.

Q: *What happened to the four hundred sons?*

A: They became stars in the sky.

Q: *How did the Hero Twins kill Alligator?*

A: They tricked him by placing a gigantic crab in a canyon at the base of a mountain. When Alligator entered the canyon to find and eat the crab, the mountain collapsed on him.

Q: *How did the Hero Twins kill Two-his-leg (Earthquake) and where did he end up?*

A: They tricked him into eating a heavy meal which made him very weak. He was buried in the ground.

EXPERT COMMENTARY

The story of these hero twins who defeat Seven Macaw makes a fascinating adventure tale even if it stands alone. Yet it is important to consider that it is a segment of a bigger story.

Professor Linda Schele from the University of Texas at Austin and Professor David Freidel, another Mayan expert, along with Professor Joy Parker suggest in their book, *Maya Cosmos*, that this tale represents a conflict between material power, represented by Seven Macaw and his jewels and beauty, and spiritual power. In other words, Seven Macaw "brightened a dark world with his beauty."[1] However, he did not have love and beauty in his heart. Without these virtues, he was a false god. When the Hero Twins rid the world of immoral beings like Seven Macaw, they pave the way for the creation of thinking, feeling human beings.

According to Schele, Freidel, and Parker, "When a Mayan king stood up . . . he wore in his headdress the fabulous plumage of birds, more often than not those of Itzam-Yeh [Seven Macaw] himself."[2] These dazzling feathers were a reminder to the king that power could be used or abused. It was up to him to plead with the gods on behalf of his people in order to keep a proper sense of balance on the Earth. "Properly used, this power preserved cosmos and country. Improperly used, like Itzam-Yeh's arrogance, it became empty strength and a danger to all around."[3]

3

THE ORIGIN OF THE SUN AND THE MOON

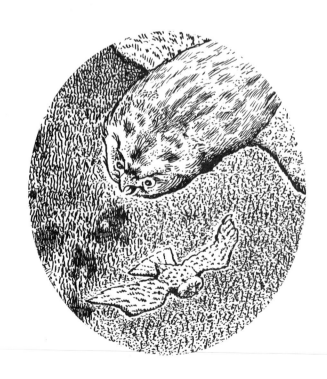

INTRODUCTION

No matter how fanatical today's sports fans are, their intensity is mild compared to that of the ancient Mayas.

The following myth takes place late in the creation saga. It concerns the heroic actions of the Hero Twins, Hunahpu and Xbalanque, and their father and uncle, Hun Hunahpu (HOON hoo-nah-POOH) and Vucub (voo-KOOB) Hunahpu. It is such a long myth that we are dividing it into two chapters. The first half takes place in Chapter 3, the conclusion in Chapter 4.

In this story, Hun Hunahpu and Vucub Hunahpu take part in a symbolic battle of the type that is common in the mythologies and religions of many cultures: A fight between good and evil, or darkness and light. In the Christian tradition, this idea is often presented in terms of a conflict between God and Satan. In this Mayan myth, the struggle is between the people of the Earth and those of the underworld, also known as the netherworld, which is the world of the dead. Like the world of the living, the underworld was home to plants, animals, and people. The Mayas believed that at sunset the underworld rotated above the Earth to become the night sky.

In many ways, this tale is a continuation of the myth told in Chapter 2. The true sun has not yet appeared on the Earth, and the twins seem to know they will have something to do with its arrival. At the same time, the final race of people will not be created until the light of the sun is up in the sky.

There are many references in the Popol Vuh to the ball game which takes place in this myth. More than just fun and games, *pohatok* was central to the Mayan religion. It was played on a court shaped like a capital I that was about 100–150 feet long and 25–50 feet wide. The court had a flat playing surface and sloping or vertical walls on two sides. Ball courts were often associated with temples, and the games were part of elaborate rituals.

Many people watched the ball games. Nobles might have watched from the temples, while ordinary people watched from on top of the walls alongside the court. People bet heavily on the games, wagering jade, gold, houses, and even slaves. Even watching the games could be risky. Not only could spectators lose if they bet on the wrong team, but the winning team might be allowed to take their clothing and jewelry. Of course, the people watching the game ran away as quickly as they could.

The penalty for losing at *pohatok* was severe. As in the Aztec game of *tlachtli*, the losing players, or at least the captain of the losing team, risked losing his head, as shown on carvings at the Mayan site of Chichen Itze. Little wonder that the Mayan word for ball court was *hom*. *Hom* is also the Mayan word for graveyard.

THE ORIGIN OF THE SUN AND THE MOON

In the land of the ancient Quiche Maya, there was a set of boy twins named Hun Hunahpu and Vucub (voo-KUB) Hunahpu. Their names referred to dates on the Mayan calendar, Hun's being "One Hunahpu," and Vucub's representing "Seven Hunahpu." The boys loved playing *pohatok* on a ball court that happened to be located on a path to the netherworld, or land of the dead. This netherworld was called Xibalba (shee-bahl-BAH), which means "place of fear."

The boys enjoyed a reputation for being the toughest *pohatok* competitors in the land. They had the best-made arm- and leg-guards and the strongest helmets, so they never injured themselves. In fact, the twins were so skilled at making the most challenging hip shots that they simply never lost a game.

However, their constant playing disturbed the Lords of Death, who lived in Xibalba and had names such as One Death, Bone Scepter, Blood Gatherer, and Pus Master.

The lords were so annoyed by the constantly resounding thumps of the bouncing balls that they decided the twins must be punished by death. To attract the twins, the lords sent four owl messengers, challenging the twins to a game of *pohatok* in Xibalba. Although their mother

begged them to say no, the twins accepted the challenge and were soon led by the owls down to Xibalba.

Making the trip to the underworld was no easy feat. The road leading to the land of the dead was an obstacle course filled with dangerous hazards. Just after they set out on their journey, the twins came upon a cliff with a steep face they had to scale down. When they reached the base of this cliff, they saw the first of three disgusting and hazardous rivers that they would have to cross.

The first river was full of floating sharp spikes. Somehow, the boys made it across without being stabbed. Next, they successfully crossed a river of blood. Finally, they had to ford a stream of flowing pus. Again, they were successful. Yet after crossing this last rancid river, the twins soon found that their ordeal was just starting.

Continuing their journey, they came to a four-way intersection. One road, called the Black Road, spoke to the twins, persuading them to follow it. Hun Hunahpu and Vucub Hunahpu did as the road told them. Eventually, they came to the throne room of Xibalba where they saw sitting figures whom, they thought, must be the Lords of Death. The twins greeted these imposing figures, but the figures did not answer. Then the twins realized the figures were only wooden mannequins, or statues, costumed to look like the Lords of Death. The Lords of Death had tricked the twins to make them look foolish.

When the lords finally stopped laughing at their prank, they offered the twins a bench where they could sit and rest. No sooner had they sat down than Hun Hunahpu and Vucub Hunahpu realized that they had been tricked again. The bench was a slab of fiery hot stone used for cooking. In pain, both boys jumped off the bench and danced around, but nothing they could do helped. The Xibalbans began to shriek with laughter as strongly as they had ever laughed before.

When they finally calmed down, the Lords of Death told the boys to go in the house where a torch and cigar would be brought to each of them. Hun Hunahpu and Vucub Hunahpu did not realize it, but these items were to play an important part in their next test. This test required that the boys keep their cigars and torches lit all night. Yet there was not enough fuel to keep either lit for very long. They were unable to complete the task to which they were assigned, so the twins were sentenced by the Lords of Death to be murdered.

The next day, the lords cut off the twins' heads and buried their bodies under the ball court in Xibalba. To show off their victory, the death lords took the head of Hun Hunahpu and stuck it in an old, dead tree as a trophy.

Suddenly, a miracle happened. The desolate tree began bearing fruit. It began to sprout calabash gourds, a fruit similar to squash. Even the head of Hun Hunahpu changed into a calabash gourd. A young underworld maiden named Xquic (sh-KIHK), or Blood Woman, heard of this magical tree and journeyed to see it. Taken in by the tree's charm, Xquic reached out her hand to pick a gourd. As soon as she did, the head of Hun Hunahpu, disguised as

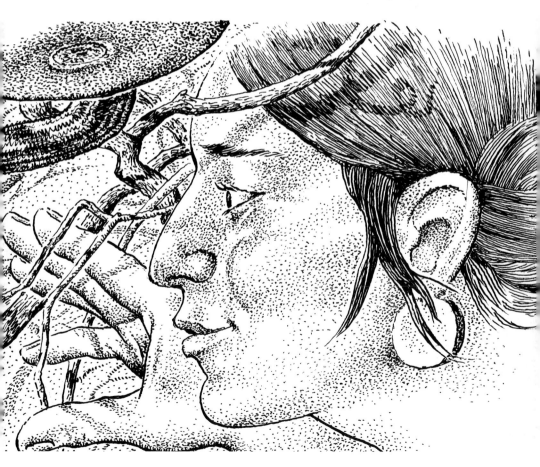

a gourd, spit into it. The spit was Hun Hunahpu's saliva, which made Xquic pregnant.

When Xquic's father noticed that his daughter was pregnant, he insisted on knowing the name of the baby's father. But Xquic could not name anyone. In response, her father announced that she had shamed him, and he demanded that she be put to death. Immediately, Xquic's father ordered messenger owls to take her away to be sacrificed. The owls were told to bring back the girl's heart in a bowl as proof that she was dead.

Xquic was desperate. She decided there was nothing to lose by telling the owls the truth—that she had become pregnant by the saliva that shot out of a gourd she had picked. The owls believed her and, because of her innocence, set her free. Having saved Xquic, the owls now wondered how to save their own lives. Xquic's father was expecting his daughter's heart in a bowl, and would be bound to punish them if they failed to obey his orders.

So the owls thought and thought and decided they could trick Xquic's father by substituting a glob of tree resin for the heart. When they returned to Xquic's father with the heart-shaped mound of tree resin in a bowl, the residents of Xibalba, thinking it was Xquic's heart, decided to burn it. When they did, the resins emitted a weird scent the Xibalbans were not familiar with. Intrigued with the intoxicating smell, they stood around gazing at the burning mass. They were so distracted, in fact, that they did not notice the messenger owls leading Xquic to freedom through a hole that led from the underworld to the Earth. Xquic had escaped, fooling all the Xibalbans in the process.

The first thing Xquic did after reaching the Earth was to pay a visit to Xmucane (sh-MOO-cane), the mother of the dead twins. Xquic convinced Xmucane that she was the widow of Hun Hunahpu, and was carrying his child. Soon however, Xquic realized she was carrying two children. Xquic gave birth to the Hero Twins, whom she named Hunahpu and Xbalanque.

As they grew, these new twin boys wanted to be great gardeners. There was one major problem; they were not very good at gardening. Every time they cleared away weeds and brush, wild animals brought more back. The boys kept trying to catch the guilty animals without much luck. Finally, they caught a rat and tried to choke and burn it to death. But the rat pleaded with the boys to be released. If they did, the rat said, he would tell them a special secret. The boys agreed that hearing this secret was worth the life of the rat.

The rodent advised the boys they were wasting their time gardening. He told them the story of their father and uncle, who were also twins, and who had been superb ballplayers. Like their father and uncle, Hunahpu and Xbalanque were destined to be great ballplayers. So the twins took the rat's advice, and in time became two of the best ballplayers around.

QUESTIONS AND ANSWERS

Q: *Why did the Lords of Death call the first set of twins down to Xibalba?*

A: The twins were making too much noise while playing *pohatok*.

Q: *What were three tests the Hero Twins had to pass in order to see the Lords of Death in Xibalba?*

A: They had to cross three disgusting rivers. One was full of floating spikes. The other two were made of blood and pus.

Q: *Name two ways the Lords of Death fooled Hun Hunahpu and Vucub Hunahpu.*

A: The Lords of Death dressed up mannequins to resemble themselves. Then they told the twins to sit on a bench, which was really a hot stone used for cooking.

Q: *Why were the Hero Twins put to death?*

A: They were killed by the Lords of Death after losing a challenge to keep their cigars and torches lit.

Q: *What happened to the head of Hun Hunahpu?*

A: It was placed in a dead tree as a trophy by the Lords of Death. Then it came to life in the form of a calabash gourd.

Q: *How was Xquic's father fooled by the messenger owls?*

A: The owls put tree resin in a bowl and claimed it was Xquic's heart.

Q: *What did the second set of twins want to be at first?*

A: The twins wanted to be gardeners.

Q: *How did the twins learn they were destined to be great ballplayers?*

A: A rat they had captured in their garden told them they should play ball instead of spending their time gardening.

EXPERT COMMENTARY

One fascinating similarity between modern religions and ancient myths is that the morals and virtues of each are often established on fields of war and during times of intense conflict. Sometimes the term *war* is a literal thing. The Old Testament is filled with battles involving the Jews and their enemies, such as the Philistines or Babylonians. The New Testament chronicles clashes between early Christians and the Romans.

For the ancient Greeks, their myths and messages were played out during the fights and skirmishes of the Trojan War. For ancient Romans, such conflicts consisted of mortal combat set up between gladiators and wild animals in coliseums. And the Mayas? Their stories of death, defeat, evil, and goodness become clear on another battlefield: the sports court. Just as many sportswriters today consider the football gridiron a kind of battlefield, the ancient Mayas' ball court was also a setting for war play. Of course, the penalty for losing the Mayan game of *pohatok* was far more severe than that of losing the Super Bowl today. By today's standards, it would also be considered inhumane.

Linda Schele is a professor at the University of Texas at Austin, and Peter Mathews is an associate professor of archaeology at the University of Calgary in Alberta, Canada. In their book, *The Code of Kings*, Schele and Mathews write,

> The ballgame was the metaphor for life and death, the arena in which players worked out fate and confronted chance. It was sometimes played for the joy of the sport, as with the Twins before the Xibalbans summoned them. The ballgame was also a metaphor for war, in which great

states and heroes strove for victory against enemies. But most of all, the Hero Twins played the ballgame as a necessary forerunner to Creation and the making of humanity. The ballcourt truly was a crevice leading into the Otherworld. When the Maya played their game, they remade Creation again and again.[1]

4

THE HERO TWINS

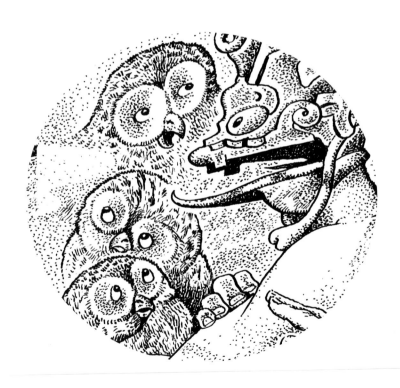

INTRODUCTION

Funerals have always been a time for religious reflection, and all religions have their own death rituals. People in many different cultures believe that when human beings die, they are reborn, are to spend eternity with their god, or are punished forever.

The Mayas feared death, even though they believed that people who had lived religious lives would go to paradise. They also believed that sacrificial victims and people who committed suicide—which they considered the greatest act of sacrifice—as well as those who died in childbirth or war would live forever in heaven. But people who were evil would suffer for eternity in Xibalba.

The Mayas decorated funerary objects, or items directly relating to a funeral, with scenes from their myths or other religious stories. It is by studying those funerary objects that many archeologists and anthropologists have learned about Mayan mythology, religion, and other important parts of day-to-day Mayan life.

Illustrations of the bats of Xibalba, animals which play an important part in the rest of this myth, were painted on numerous funerary vases. Many of these paintings are seen on vases found in locales within the Mayan empire, where legend has it that the Hero Twins, Hunahpu and Xbalanque, entered the dark netherworld of Xibalba. In certain cases, bats' eyes are depicted on their wings and collar.[1] This may be because bats have long been thought to be blind. In fact, they are not, although they do primarily use their hearing and not their sight to orient themselves.

Scholars have uncovered other funerary vases with

paintings depicting the death lords of Xibalba. Some wear yokes, equipment worn when playing *pohatok*, on their hips. Others have been portrayed smoking a cigar or sitting on a jaguar skin. Still others show Hunahpu and Xbalanque about to sacrifice themselves, an action which plays an important role in the rest of this myth.

THE HERO TWINS

Like their father and uncle, Hunahpu and Xbalanque made a lot of noise when they played *pohatok*. And like their father and uncle, one day they disturbed the Lords of Death down in Xibalba. As before, the lords called on the owl messengers to bring the new set of twins to their home in the underworld.

On their way to Xibalba, the boys had to travel over the same route their father and uncle had taken. They lowered themselves down the cliff, and passed across the rivers of spikes, blood, and pus. However, when they came to the four-way intersection, they avoided making the same mistake as their ancestors.

These twins had a plan. Hunahpu pulled a hair from his skin and turned it into a mosquito. They told the mosquito to fly on ahead and bite all the Lords of Death. The mosquito did as he was told. First, he bit the wooden mannequins that were dressed as the Lords of Death. When the mannequins did not react, the mosquito knew they were not real people. So the mosquito looked further until he discovered the real death lords. Then he bit one after another.

As each death lord was bitten, he called out in pain. The Lord of Death standing closest to the one who had been bitten would call out the bitten lord's name and ask him what the matter was. For example, just after Pus Master was bitten, Blood Gatherer responded, "What is it, Pus Master?" Then, after Blood Gatherer was bitten, the death lord next to him asked, "What is it, Blood Gatherer?" This process continued throughout the entire line of the Lords of Death. The twins paid careful attention to this ritual, and soon they knew the name of every single Lord of Death.

Therefore, when the boys arrived in the underworld throne room, they were able to greet each lord by his given name. They made sure to tell the lords that they would

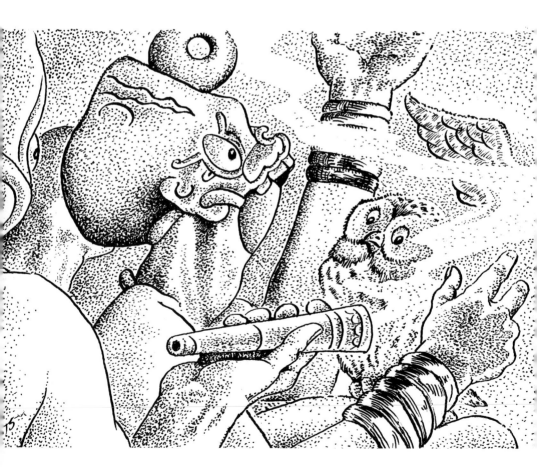

never greet wooden mannequins. The Lords of Death were impressed with the twins' knowledge. When Hunahpu and Xbalanque were instructed to take a seat on the hot stone slab that had burned their relatives, the twins knew better and refused. The Lords of Death were amazed that the twins knew all their tricks.

Now the Lords of Death began the most difficult challenges. The twins were given a series of dangerous tests. Each took place in a different room called a "house." In the House of Gloom, Hunahpu and Xbalanque were given the same cigar and torch that their ancestors had

received, and were told to keep both objects lit all night long. The twins outsmarted the Lords of Death by placing a macaw's red tail feathers on the torch and fireflies on the ends of the cigars. In the morning, when the lords checked the twins' progress, they were stunned. The torch and cigars seemed as if they were still burning. The twins had passed the first challenge.

Next, they were sent to the House of Razors, which was filled with sharp knives. The knives were supposed to cut the boys into pieces, but the twins convinced the knives that their job was to cut only animals. The next challenge was the House of Jaguars, where they faced a room full of ferocious wild cats. Hunahpu and Xbalanque distracted the jaguars by feeding them bones. Next, they survived the House of Cold and the House of Fire, where they were put to the test of severe temperatures.

One more test remained: The House of Bats. These flying rodents had knives instead of noses. To escape the bats, the twins hid inside a pair of hollow blowguns. All night long, they stayed inside their safe havens and heard the bats flying all around them. But as the darkness began to fade, Hunahpu could no longer resist the temptation to peek out to see if dawn was breaking. Just as he stuck his head out of his blowgun, a vicious bat sliced it off, and it went rolling onto the underworld's ball court. The Lords of Death cheered and celebrated what seemed to be a victory over one of the twins.

Now, Xbalanque had an idea. As dawn was approaching, he called on all the animals to bring him their favorite foods. The *coati* (KOH-ah-tee), which was similar to a raccoon, brought Xbalanque a round squash, which he placed atop his brother's neck. With great skill, Xbalanque then carved the squash so it resembled Hunahpu's head and face. Miraculously, the squash became a working head for Hunahpu. Then the twins walked over to the netherworld ball court, where the death lords challenged them to a game of *pohatok*.

Before the game began, Hunahpu and Xbalanque asked a rabbit to hide in some nearby trees. When the game started, the twins saw that one of the Lords of Death was using Hunahpu's real head as the ball. As Hunahpu's head was bouncing around the court, Xbalanque batted it toward the trees where the rabbit was hiding. The rabbit pounced from the trees and began hopping across the ball court. The death lords mistook the rabbit for the bouncing ball and chased after it. While they were gone, Xbalanque grabbed his brother's real head and placed it back on his brother's body. Then he took the squash and tossed it into play on the ball court.

As soon as the Lords of Death returned from chasing the rabbit, they tried kicking the squash, thinking it was Hunahpu's head. The squash splattered open, its seeds spilling in all directions. With no ball, the Lords of Death had to concede defeat. Hunahpu and Xbalanque had won.

However, the story did not end there. The twins called on two prophets named Xulu (SHOO-loo) and Pacam (pah-KAM) to ask what they should do next. The prophets told the boys that although they had managed to survive all the tricks and games offered up by the Lords of Death, they were still destined to die. The prophets revealed that this outcome was all part of a grand plan.

The Lords of Death came up with one more test. This time, they built a fiery hot oven and challenged the boys to jump over it safely four times. By now, Hunahpu and Xbalanque knew what they must do. They jumped headfirst into the fire, burning themselves to death. The Xibalbans happily took the boys' bones from the fire, ground them into fine powder, and scattered the dust in a river.

Even in death, the Hero Twins were not out of miracles. Instead of floating away, their powdery bones sank to the river bottom. In five days, the boys came back to life as catfish. On the sixth day, they took on their previous human forms, but now they were dressed as vagrants who danced and performed magic tricks for a living.

Word of the performances of these two unknown vagabonds reached the Lords of Death, who announced that they wanted a special show just for them.

So the Hero Twins danced and performed supernatural tricks in the palace of the Lords of Death. One death lord asked the twins to sacrifice a dog and bring it back to life. They accomplished that trick easily. A second death lord asked them to do the same thing with a human. Xbalanque cut off Hunahpu's head, dug out his heart, then commanded him to stand up. He did so easily, and the Xibalbans were amazed. Then the Death Lords called for an even more daring trick. They begged to be sacrificed.

So Hunahpu and Xbalanque did as they were told. They sacrificed the two death lords. It was the same trick they had performed with the dog and with Hunahpu. However, this time they did not bring their victims back to life. The Lords of Death remained dead. The remaining Lords of Death were furious and demanded to know why this time the trick had not worked.

Then Hunahpu and Xbalanque stepped out of their disguises and addressed the lords: "We have avenged our father, One Hunahpu, and his brother, Seven Hunahpu, and now we will kill you."[2]

The rest of the Xibalbans begged for their lives. The twins made a deal. If the residents of Xibalba would tell them where their father and uncle were buried, there would be no more killing. The Xibalbans agreed to the proposal, and they were spared. However, they would never be powerful again. With the information supplied by the Xibalbans, the Hero Twins located their father and uncle and brought them back to life. Hunahpu and Xbalanque assured their elders that they would always be respected and prayed to.

The twins had one last journey to make. They ascended to the heavens, where they took their places as the sun and the moon, lighting up the world for eternity. From then on, whenever the people looked up at the sky, they would remember the valor and ingeniousness of the Hero Twins.

QUESTIONS AND ANSWERS

Q: *How did the Hero Twins avoid being fooled by the Lords of Death?*

A: The twins sent a mosquito ahead to bite the false mannequins who resembled the Lords of Death. When the mannequins did not react, the twins knew they were not real.

Q: *How did the Hero Twins meet the challenge of the Lords of Death when asked to keep their cigars and torch lit all night?*

A: They placed a macaw's red tail feathers on the torch and fireflies on the ends of the cigars.

Q: *Name the five houses in which the Hero Twins faced death challenges.*

A: The House of Razors; the House of Jaguars; the House of Cold; the House of Fire; and the House of Bats.

Q: *What mistake did Hunahpu make that allowed a bat to successfully attack him?*

A: He peeked out of his blowgun to see if dawn was breaking.

Q: *What did the Lords of Death first use as the ball during their ball game with the hero twins, and how was it returned to its proper place?*

A: Hunahpu's head was used first as a ball. The twins placed a hopping rabbit on the court, which distracted the Lords of Death. While the Lords of Death were away, Xbalanque placed Hunahpu's real head back on his body.

Q: *How did the Hero Twins trick the Lords of Death into allowing themselves to be sacrificed?*

A: They disguised themselves as vagabonds who danced and performed magic tricks. The Lords of Death commanded them to sacrifice a dog and bring it back to life, and the Hero Twins easily accomplished that. The death lords then demanded that they do the same with a human. When the Hero Twins succeeded with that, as well, the Lords of Death begged to be sacrificed. The Hero Twins did as they were asked—but did not bring the Lords of Death back to life, thereby avenging the deaths of their father and uncle.

Q: *What did the Hero Twins become after killing the Lords of Death?*

A: They ascended into Heaven and became the sun and moon.

EXPERT COMMENTARY

In their book, *A Forest of Kings*, professors Linda Schele and David Freidel noted three basic themes of classic Mayan religion, which appear in this myth. Basically, they concern intelligence, skill, and the giving of one's self.

Schele and Freidel write that the Hero Twins did not conquer the Lords of Death with their muscles. Instead, they used their wits to outsmart them. The boys found clever ways to keep their cigars and torch lit, and tricked the death lords into sacrificing themselves.

The two authors write:

> Secondly, resurrection and rebirth came through sacrifice—especially death by decapitation. The hero twins were conceived when the severed head of their father spit into the hand of their mother. They defeated death by submitting to decapitation and sacrifice.[3]

In another book, entitled *Maya Cosmos*, Freidel, Schele, and Joy Parker state that the Hero Twins' death was their last and greatest accomplishment. They state:

> "The greatest of their tricks was to submit knowingly to defeat and sacrifice in order to win the larger game."[4] The "larger game" was, of course, eternal life as the sun and moon.

Another scholar, Michael D. Coe, in the sixth edition of his book, *The Maya*, states that the death and resurrection of the Hero Twins is also a metaphor for an important part of the Mayan way of life, farming, and their staff of life, maize. Coe, a retired professor of anthropology at Yale

University in New Haven, Connecticut, expands on the conclusions of another expert when he writes:

> As Karl Taube has shown, the parallel with the agricultural cycle is patent in this myth. When the farmer plants his milpa, he sends the maize into the Underworld down the hole he has made with his digging stick; then, with the coming of the rains, the maize is 'resurrected' as a young sprout.[5]

5

THE CREATION OF THE WORLD

INTRODUCTION

Because the Aztecs belonged to different tribes and lived in varied locales, they collected many colorful creation myths. Some differed only slightly from one another; others showed great contradictions. However, one element common to most Aztec creation myths was the gods' desire for human blood. In fact, like the Mayas, the Aztecs demanded human as well as animal sacrifice.

Despite a superior knowledge of astronomy, the Aztecs believed that the sun revolved around the Earth. One of their strongest fears was that the sun might someday stop turning and freeze in place in the sky. If that happened, they reasoned, the unending rays of the sun would burn everything on Earth, thereby making it impossible for the planet to support life. They believed that the only way to keep the sun from stopping in its place was to provide the sun god, Hultzilopochtli, with human hearts and blood.

Many of the sacrificial victims were prisoners of war, and as the power of the Aztecs grew, they captured and sacrificed increasing numbers of people. However, once a year, the Aztecs chose a boy to be sacrificed. For a full year before he was sacrificed, this young man impersonated the great god Tezcatlipoca. He was given servants to attend to his every wish. He wore the best clothes and was trained in music and religion. A month before he was to be sacrificed, the boy was married to four virgins who sang and danced with him around the city. For five days before his sacrifice, the people feasted and celebrated.

The actual sacrifice was part of a solemn ceremony. Just before he met his death, the boy was rowed in a canoe to a temple. He was then led up a series of steps to the temple summit. As he walked up the stairs, he first played, then destroyed, a series of ceremonial flutes. At the top, a group of attending Aztec priests tied the boy to the altar and cut out his heart, which was offered to the sun to keep the celestial body moving through the heavens.

THE CREATION
OF THE WORLD

The world we live in today is not the only world that ever existed. At least, that is true, according to the ancient Aztecs.

The Aztecs believed that before our current world was created, there were four worlds, called suns. Although the four worlds were created, none was perfect.

The first world began when the powerful god, Tezcatlipoca (tes-CAHT-li-PO-kah) turned himself into the sun. The people of this first sun were giants who survived the heat of their habitat by living in the shade of massive trees and eating a vegetarian diet of corn, berries, and acorns, with which Tezcatlipoca and other gods had provided them. The giant citizens of this first world were so powerful, it was said, that they could lift trees out of the ground with their bare hands.

Another powerful god, Quetzalcoatl (ket-SAHL-koh-AHTL), who was a jealous rival of Tezcatlipoca, was angry that Tezcatlipoca was ruling the world. Quetzalcoatl took many forms, but was often described as having a light complexion and a beard. Quetzalcoatl started a fight with Tezcatlipoca and continued to battle him until he knocked Tezcatlipoca out of the sky. Tezcatlipoca was furious for being dethroned. In response, Tezcatlipoca changed himself into a jaguar and demolished the entire world, including all the giant people and the sun.

But Tezcatlipoca's powers were not strong enough to destroy Quetzalcoatl, and he survived the end of the first sun. He then created a second world with a race of people who lived on a diet of pine nuts. This time, Tezcatlipoca gained revenge against Quetzalcoatl by literally kicking him out of the sky. Tezcatlipoca then created a wind so huge that it swept away the sun which had shown so brightly. The wind also killed most of the people, and those who survived were turned into monkeys. Their ancestors can be seen today swinging from trees in the wild forests.

The third world began with the actions of the god of rain, Tlaloc, who had big, bulging eyes and giant teeth. Tlaloc transformed himself into the sun and became ruler of the world. Again, Quetzalcoatl was unhappy, and sent a series of floods to wash away the Earth. People who lived through the horrible floods were turned into birds. The fourth world was the product of Tlaloc's wife, Chalchiuhtlicue (chal-CHEE-ooh-tlee-quay), who became the sun in her husband's place. Yet another flood destroyed this world, and those people who survived became fish.

For a fourth time, there was complete darkness. At this point, the gods had a meeting and decided that one god had to sacrifice himself to become the new sun. A homely and modest god named Nanautzin (nah-nah-WAH-tsin) volunteered to do the job. The ugly Nanautzin, whose body was deformed and whose skin was covered with sickening sores, was surprised to be accepted. The other gods had always treated him like an outcast. However, Nanautzin confessed he would be happy to be of use and sacrifice himself if it meant that a fifth world could be brought into existence.

The gods thought over Nanautzin's offer, but they agreed that the job was too big for just one god to accomplish. A handsome, wealthy god volunteered to join Nanautzin in the self-sacrifice. The rest of the gods accepted his offer.

Over the next several days, the gods built a pyramid of stone with a bonfire on its top. The handsome god was asked to jump into the fire. He tried four times, but each time he lost his nerve and backed away from the scorching flames. Finally, he told the other gods he would not be able to keep his promise.

Then the gods asked Nanautzin to leap into the raging bonfire. Nanautzin mustered up all the courage he could and sprang into the searing flames. As his body burned, the sun began to light up the sky. Seeing the power Nanautzin had displayed, the rich god decided that he must somehow find a way to imitate Nanautzin's bravery. So he, too, jumped into the blaze. Still, Nanautzin received most of the glory from the other gods since he never acted cowardly during the entire episode.

Although there was now a life-giving sun in the sky, the Earth did not exist as we know it today. Between the heavens and the water below, all that existed was a huge monster goddess named Tlaltecuhtli (Ta-lal-TECK-oot-lee). She was a vicious beast with several mouths all over her body—all of them filled with sharp teeth. Tlaltecuhtli ate anything in her path.

The two mightiest gods, Quetzalcoatl and Tezcatlipoca, agreed they could not create the Earth with this hideous monster around. They told each other that they must find some way to stop that goddess from destroying everything they created.

Then, they came up with a plan. They turned themselves into giant snakes and wrapped themselves

around Tlaltecuhtli. Together they pulled, stretching Tlaltecuhtli until her body broke in two. The top half of her body, including her head, became the Earth. The force of the break tossed her bottom half into the air, and it became the heavens.

To thank Tlaltecuhtli for her sacrifice, Quetzalcoatl and Tezcatlipoca decided to give her a special gift. From then on, she would provide people with all the natural wonders they would need to live. Her hair became trees, herbs, and flowers. Her skin was transformed into grass and flowers. Her eyes were turned into small caves, wells, and fountains, while large caves and rivers were crafted from her many mouths. From her shoulders, mountains were created, and her nose was transformed into smaller hills and valleys.

However, Tlaltecuhtli remained unhappy. Often she could be heard screaming in the night, craving human blood. Only when human lives were given up to her would she continue to produce nature's needs for other living humans.

So now, the heavens existed and the Earth looked like the one we live on today. Yet there were no people. One day, the great god Quetzalcoatl journeyed to the underworld, the land of the dead, to bring back the bones of the people who had lived in the fourth sun. But the underworld, known as Mictlan (MICK-t'lan) and ruled by a sinister skeleton god named Mictlantecuhtli (MICK-t'lan-tee-coot'lee), was a dangerous place. As soon as he entered Mictlan, Quetzalcoatl discovered the bones of his father, which he wanted to take back to the Earth.

The mischievous Mictlantecuhtli was not going to make this easy. As Quetzalcoatl was about to leave Mictlan with his father's bones, Mictlantecuhtlui's servants stopped him and ordered him to leave the bones where they were. Quetzalcoatl did not know what to do, so he asked his animal spirit form, called a *nahual*, to advise him. The *nahual* told Quetzalcoatl to pretend to leave the bones. Then, once the servants returned to their master, he was to pack the bones and take them with him.

Quetzalcoatl followed his *nahual's* instructions. Carefully, he wrapped up the bones and set out for the Earth. But Mictlantecuhtl was not finished yet with his rival. He demanded that his servants dig a hole to trap Quetzalcoatl. As he made a hurried escape, Quetzalcoatl tripped and fell into the hole. A flock of vicious birds appeared, scaring him and causing him to drop the bones. The birds then landed on Quetzalcoatl's treasured package and ferociously pecked at it until the wrapping was shredded and the bones were shattered into powdery pieces.

In distress, Quetzalcoatl called out to his *nahual* again. His *nahual* urged him to continue on his quest. This time, Quetzalcoatl was successful. Quetzalcoatl brought the powdered bones to Cihuacoatl, the goddess of childbirth, who ground them into the flour. Quetzalcoatl's blood was added to the newly-made flour, and the mixture of blood and bones came to life as a new race of human beings.

However, Quetzalcoatl warned his newly-made human beings that the current world might not be permanent. If the people became wicked, this world would one day be destroyed.

QUESTIONS AND ANSWERS

Q: *According to this creation myth, how many worlds were there before the current one was created?*

A: The myth says there were four worlds before the current one.

Q: *Why were the previous worlds destroyed?*

A: One god would become jealous of another god's power and destroy his world.

Q: *What became of the people who survived the great winds that destroyed the second world?*

A: They were turned into monkeys.

Q: *What happened to the people who managed to survive the great floods which ruined the third world?*

A: Those people became birds.

Q: *How does the god Nanautzin become transformed into the sun?*

A: He jumps into a sacrificial fire, and as his body burns, the sun begins to light up the sky.

Q: *From what materials were human beings created?*

A: Humans were made from a combination of bones and blood.

Q: *According to this myth, what will happen if people today begin acting wickedly?*

A: The current world will be destroyed, just like the previous four.

EXPERT COMMENTARY

The *nahual*, or *nagual*, is a personal guardian spirit which some Mesoamericans believe lives in animals such as deer, jaguar, or birds. The *nahual*, which plays an important part in the creation of human beings, is a fascinating concept. However, it is not only found in Aztec literature. Similar concepts are found in the mythology of native North Americans. In addition, Hindus believe in a closely related concept, called an *avatar*. To the Hindus, the *avatar* is an earthly form of a god, which can take the form of a human being or an animal.

British mythologist Veronica Ions, in her book, *The World's Mythology in Colour*, explains that the *nahual* took different forms. Some Aztec heroes could actually take the form of their *nahual*, and travel disguised from one location to another to perform what could seem like magic. Indeed, a *nahual* could even take on the form of a nonliving act of nature, such as rain, clouds, and lightning.[1]

Still, to most figures, such as Quetzalcoatl in this creation myth, the *nahual* was a special helpmate that guided living beings in their troubled times. When a person died, his personal *nahual* died, too.

Ions adds:

> Just as the nagual [sic] died with the individual to which it was attached, so the sun of a given era was thought to perish with the degeneration of a species. Thus the present sun was said to be the fifth, born of all four elements, its predecessors having sprung separately from Earth, Air, Fire and Water.[2]

Ions further explains that for the sun to continue shining on Earth, human beings must continue to do good. They must make efforts to gain wisdom and freedom and must sacrifice both in reality and in prayer. She notes that this "was shown too in the continued search of the gods for a species capable of appreciating and praising their creator, and thus nourish and sustain their gods."[3]

Another scholar with a noteworthy analysis is Elizabeth Hill Boone, a professor and museum curator based at Dumbarton Oaks, a well-respected museum and research center in Washington, D.C. Boone notes how Nanautzin's courageous act sums up the Aztecs' devotion to religion and sacrifice. In her book, *The Aztec World*, Boone writes:

> First, Nanahuatzin (sic) boldly offered himself on the fire in order to become the sun; then, all the other deities gave their own lives to set it moving on its course. Just as the gods had surrendered their hearts to the sacrificial blade, the Aztecs believed humans must give their hearts to keep the sun and moon in motion. It became their mission as a chosen people to give the sun strength to fight its way across the heavens each day, and to battle its way across the underworld each night. It was their mission, too, to satisfy the earth's hunger for human hearts and thereby give her the strength to bear fruit. This sense of divine mission was at the core of Aztec religious zeal.[4]

6

FEEDING THE AZTEC PEOPLE

INTRODUCTION

Enter a Mexican restaurant today and you will find that many of the items on the menu are made from one food staple: corn, called *maiz* in Spanish and also known as maize. Maize grows in abundance in Mexico today, as it has for centuries. In fact, one of the most common bread products eaten in Mexico today is the corn tortilla.

Corn pollen grains thousands of years old have been found growing in rocks below Mexico City. In the state of New Mexico, just north of the country of Mexico, corncobs were discovered in a cave that is thought to be 5,600 years old.[1]

As it was to the Mayas, maize was the life force of the Aztecs. It was their main source of sustenance, and without it they could not have survived. Though the Aztecs may not have known it, corn also kept them healthy. It is a hearty source of B vitamins, potassium, fiber and vitamins C and A. In fact, the more yellow the corn, the more vitamin A it has. White corn has other nutrients, but it is lacking in vitamin A.

Considering its importance, it was only natural that the Aztecs would consider corn a gift from the gods. The following tale tells the story of how the great god Quetzalcoatl brought corn to the Aztec people. And this story also tells how Quetzalcoatl brought another important plant to the Aztecs. That plant is called *maguey* (mag-WAY).

Maguey was almost as important to the Aztecs as corn. Once it is pruned, the maguey plant produces endless shoots, and the Aztecs used it in many ways. They made needles from its thorns and cloth from its fibers. From its leaves, they made roofing material for homes, paper, and even food. But one of *maguey's* most important uses was to provide an alcoholic drink called *pulque* (POOL-kay).

Made from the fermented sap of the *maguey* plant, *pulque* was an important part of Aztecs religious ceremonies. Sometimes it was drunk during rituals; other times it was sacrificed to the gods.

According to legend, Quetzalcoatl gave *maguey* to the Aztecs because he thought they needed more pleasure in their lives. Because the *pulque* made from the *maguey* plant was fermented, those who drank it often became intoxicated. However, this did not mean that anybody could become drunk at will. Among the Aztecs, becoming drunk in public was a severe crime, which carried stiff penalties. A member of the nobility who was drunk in public often faced a death sentence. Only elders who were well respected by Aztec society were permitted to indulge in *pulque* publicly.

FEEDING THE AZTEC PEOPLE

Now that human beings had been created for the fifth new world, they would need to eat in order to survive. So Quetzalcoatl and the other gods went exploring to find some way to feed this new race of people.

One day Quetzalcoatl spotted an ant carrying a big kernel of maize. Right away, he knew that this unusual food would be ideal to feed humans. Quetzalcoatl wanted to know where the ant got the corn. At first he simply asked the ant, but the ant refused to answer. However, after repeated questioning, the ant agreed to take the god to the place where the corn grew, Mount Tonacatepetl (ton-ah-cah-TAPE-etel), or the "mountain of sustenance." Quetzalcoatl then turned himself into an ant. That way he could follow the other ant into very small places to where the maize might be hidden.

The ant led the god into the recesses of Mount Tonacatepetl, where maize was growing in abundance. Quetzalcoatl also discovered beans, peppers, and all sorts of other foods which could be eaten by humankind.

Still in the form of an ant, Quetzalcoatl grabbed a kernel of corn and took it back to the humans to plant. He then informed the other gods of his wondrous discovery, and gleefully told them that he had also seen many other foods on Mount Tonacatepetl that could sustain people.

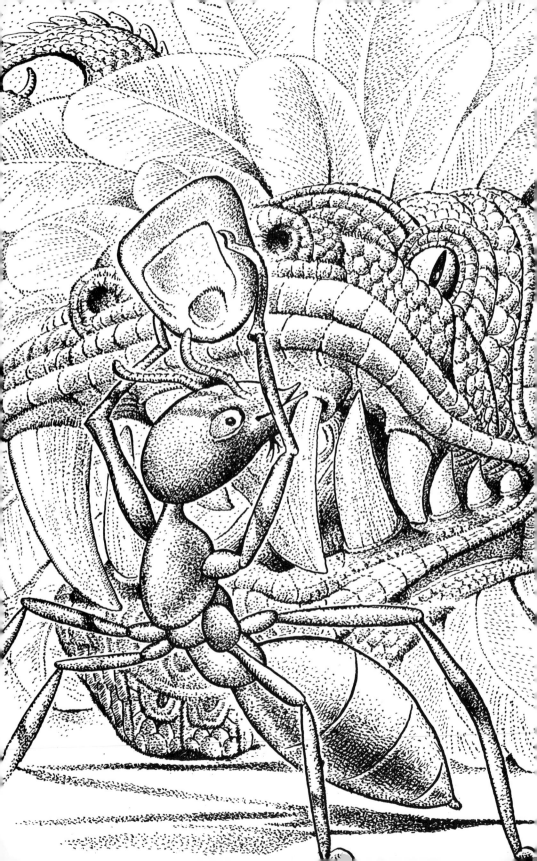

However, there was one big problem: How could all this food growing in abundance deep inside a big mountain be brought to the people? After all, only a creature as small as an ant would be able to reach the tempting supply of food.

Nonetheless, Quetzalcoatl embarked on a plan. He looped a giant rope around all of Mount Tonacatepetl and tried to pull the mountain to where the people lived. Since the mountain was so big, it would not budge, despite the god's great powers. So he asked the other gods for suggestions. A wise old pair of gods named Oxomoco (oh-shoh-MOH-ko) and Cipactonal (si-pak-TOH-nal) gave the problem a great deal of thought. They decided that the answer was to break open the mountain, allowing men and women to have easy access to the food inside. So with all their combined power, the gods split open the rock that made up Mount Tonacatepetl and the huge bounty of food now appeared within reach of the people.

But there was one more problem. Opening the rock had angered the god of rain, Tlaloc. With great speed, Tlaloc and his children grabbed all the corn and other food from the inside of the mountain and took it with them before any people could get to it. To this day, Tlaloc, the rain god, gives back the food to people only in amounts he sees fit to allow. Some years, when there is the right amount of rain, he is generous. Other times, when there is too much rain, he teases the people with an overabundance of food, which rots before their eyes. When there is too little rain, Tlaloc acts selfishly by causing a shortage of the people's staple food.

Although people now had food to keep them alive, the gods felt there was something missing. The human beings worked and survived, but nothing seemed to bring great happiness to their lives. What could be done?

Quetzalcoatl felt they needed something stronger in

their diets. He decided to contact beautiful young Mayahuel, the goddess of the *maguey*. Mayahuel lived in the sky with her evil grandmother, who was a *tzitzimitl*, a female demon who takes the shape of stars and represents evil in the world. Every morning, Mayahuel's grandmother and her sister *tzitzimime* threaten to destroy the world by doing battle against the sun.

Mayahuel and her grandmother were sleeping when Quetzalcoatl arrived in their sky-house. He woke Mayahuel and convinced her to come with him to Earth. Upon reaching Earth together, they took the form of a large, two-limbed tree, each becoming a branch.

As soon as the grandmother awoke, she discovered that her precious Mayahuel was missing. In a fit of anger, the grandmother asked the rest of the *tzitzimime* to lead her to Earth to find her granddaughter. The evil star demons zoomed to Earth and immediately found the tree where Mayahuel and Quetzalcoatl were hiding. Just as the demons arrived, the tree broke in half and the branches fell flat on the hard ground.

Outraged at her granddaughter for running away, Mayahuel's grandmother viciously attacked the branch, breaking it into pieces. Then she allowed the other *tzitzimime* to further demolish the branch before eating parts of Mayahuel. When finished, the *tzitzimime* returned to their home in the sky. Quetzalcoatl, who was never touched by the *tzitzimime*, converted himself into his usual god-like form. Quetzalcoatl made a simple grave for Mayahuel by burying her bare bones in a spot on the Earth. From her burial site, the first *maguey* plant grew. And from that *maguey* plant, the first *pulque* was made.

QUESTIONS AND ANSWERS

Q: *How did Quetzalcoatl first attempt to get the corn that is growing inside Mount Tonacatepetl to the people?*

A: He tied a giant rope around the mountain and tried to pull it to where the people lived.

Q: *How did the gods finally get the corn and other foods growing inside the mountain to the people?*

A: The gods used their powers to split open the mountain.

Q: *How does this story explain why different amounts of rain fall during different years today?*

A: When the mountain was split open, Tlaloc, the god of rain, became angry. He and his children grabbed all the food from inside the mountain and kept it. He gives the food back as he wishes.

Q: *Why did Quetzalcoatl decide to contact Mayahuel?*

A: He felt people needed something in their diets to make them happy. Quetzalcoatl believed Mayahuel might help him learn what that might be.

Q: *What is the importance of the tree with two limbs?*

A: Together, Mayahuel and Quetzalcoatl created the tree and turned themselves into two branches so they could hide from Mayahuel's grandmother and the other *tzitzimime*.

Q: *From what spot did the first* maguey *plant grow?*

A: Mayahuel's burial site.

EXPERT COMMENTARY

In the *Encyclopedia of World Religions*, it is explained how corn, or maize, went beyond being a simple food to become a part of the spiritual attitudes of the Aztecs.

> The almost passive center of the farmers' religion was the maize plant . . . maize was life, and the rhythm of planting and reaping conditioned the whole concept of the meaning of the passage of time in Mexico.[2]

When the green ears of corn first began to appear in spring, it was cause for celebration. Richard F. Townsend, a professor at the University of Chicago, wrote in *The Aztecs*:

> Maize was portrayed in feminine terms, and three deities were especially important. Xilonen, "young maize," was portrayed as an adolescent girl with the first tender corn of the rainy season harvest worn on her headdress. Chicomecoatl, "seven serpent," was the title given to dried seed corn, which was harvested and kept for the next year; priestesses bearing ears of this seed corn appeared at the onset of the planting season. Cinteotl (Sin-tay-otl), "sacred maize-ear," was the more general term for corn eaten after the first harvest season.[3]

Maize harvest time was cause for a religious ceremony. Ears of maize were bundled up to represent Cinteotl and were stored in places of honor—special granaries where they would be kept until the sowing of the seeds the following spring. At the harvest fiesta, girls wore headbands and necklaces of popcorn dyed in festive colors. Meanwhile, priests performed a kind of religious magic so that each year the maize would be protected from bugs, diseases, and its other natural enemies.

The *Encyclopedia of World Religions* says that the Aztecs worshipped maize as if it "were the most delightful of flowers, and indeed so it was."[4]

7

THE CREATION OF MUSIC

INTRODUCTION

Throughout human history, people have celebrated, entertained, and comforted one another with music. The Aztecs were no exception. In fact, music was so important to the Aztecs that they claimed the gods had a major role in bringing it to the people. According to the following Aztec myth, it took two gods who were commonly at odds with each other, Quetzalcoatl and Tezcatlipoca, to work together to take music from its home in the heavens and bring it to Earth.

Just as we do today, the Aztecs used music in every part of their lives, from solemn religious ceremonies to happy times of leisure. In fact, it would have been difficult to find any time of the day when music was not calming or exciting the Aztec people.

Aztec ceremonies often involved singing and dancing. The Aztecs respected professional singers and dancers, who were accompanied by professional orchestras that played during and after religious events. Their instruments, made from materials such as stone, wood, seashells, and squash gourds, included flutes, horns, whistles, and drums.

The singers and dancers performed while the orchestra played in the background, and often the dancers themselves served as musicians. On their clothes, they wore natural noisemakers, like rattles made from bones and seashells. As they danced, these materials sounded like percussion instruments.

Musicians also rendered their melodious sounds at feasts and banquets, many of which took place immediately following serious religious ceremonies. Sometimes music was played simply to entertain those gathered for an occasion. Other times, flutes and drums were used to provide the background for plays and poetry readings. Indeed, music was so beloved that some nobles and other wealthy people kept private orchestras in their homes. However, the Aztec emperor Montezuma II, the ninth Aztec king, who was killed in 1520 A.D. when the Spanish invaders came, had little patience for imperfect musicians. It is said that he sentenced to prison any singer who could not stick to the proper key or any musician who skipped a beat.

The following myth, "The Creation of Music," was originally written in the Aztecs' language as a poem with a rhythmical and lyrical cadence, like the words to a song.

THE CREATION OF
MUSIC

The gods agreed that the fifth and present world was a beautiful place. The many parts of Tlaltecuhtli, the earth monster, had been splendidly transformed to make the most wonderful sights. There were vibrant flowers, gushing rivers, lush woods, and refreshing streams. This new Earth was also home to majestic mountains and rambling meadows. There were truly enough natural marvels for all the people of Earth to enjoy.

The gods enjoyed the sights, too, until one day when Tezcatlipoca looked around the Earth and complained that something was missing. Animals could roar and people could talk, but there was no music. Tezcatlipoca said that music could delight the soul like nothing else.

So Tezcatlipoca set out to find a way to bring music to the world. His first task was to contact Quetzalcoatl to see if the great god could assist him. At that time, the feathered serpent god had taken the form of Wind. The sound of blowing leaves and creaking tree limbs let Tezcatlipoca know that Quetzalcoatl, in the form of Wind, was on his way to see him.

When Tezcatlipoca found Quetzalcoatl, he asked him to embark on a special trip, which was to begin at the ocean's edge. There, Quetzalcoatl would find three of Tezcatlipoca's servants: Water Woman; Water Monster; and a third servant named Cane-and-Conch. Quetzalcoatl would need to order the three servants to make him a bridge reaching to the Sun, for it was in the house of Sun that talented musicians and singers lived. Once he had entered the house of Sun, Quetzalcoatl would be able to select the best musicians and singers and bring them back to their new home on Earth.

So Quetzalcoatl did as he was told. At the beach he found the three servants Tezcatlipoca had mentioned. The trio successfully built the bridge to the house of Sun, and Quetzalcoatl proceeded to climb the bridge until he reached the Sun.

Upon arriving in this new land, Quetzalcoatl found musicians of all stripes, each wearing a different kind of uniform that reflected his own specialty. The musicians who played lullabies and songs for small children wore white clothing. Wandering minstrels who played as they roamed among the clouds were garbed in a vivid shade of blue. Music makers who bathed in the warm rays of the Sun while playing their flutes dressed in sparkling yellow. Others who liked to play musical stories about love donned clothing that was red as a big, juicy cherry.

One thing Quetzalcoatl noticed was that there were no

musicians wearing a dark or depressing color. The reason for that was simple: there were no sad songs being played in the house of Sun.

Sun enjoyed all his musicians, and was not willing to let any of them go. As soon as he realized that Quetzalcoatl, in the form of Wind, had made this visit to recruit his musicians and bring them to Earth, Sun told his tune makers to be silent. As long as they made no sounds, Quetzalcoatl, or Wind, would not be able to locate them.

Wind called for the musicians to come with him to Earth, yet they made not a sound. Again and again he ordered them to follow him, but they did not play even a single note. Nor did they move even one step.

Back on Earth, Tezcatlipoca was becoming so angered by the musicians' disobedience that he decided to scare them into leaving the house of Sun. With all his power, Tezcatlipoca turned the skies into a raging mass of black clouds, lightning, and thunder. Sun was first surrounded, then swallowed up by the sinister, dark storm clouds. Again, wind urged all the musicians to come with him, and this time they flew towards him. Wind gently caressed the musicians, protecting them in his arms as he carried them to Earth. There, the musicians were welcomed by every living thing—the people, the animals, the flowers, and the trees.

Once on Earth, the song crafters taught everyone how to play their soothing music. Human beings were not the only ones to learn the musicians' secrets, however. Music was also heard throughout the world in the chirping of birds, the roar of the ocean's waves, and the rushing waters of a mountain stream. From then on, music of all kinds would inspire, soothe, entertain, energize, and calm all the beings on Earth.

QUESTIONS AND ANSWERS

Q: *When Quetzalcoatl says, "Earth is sick with sadness," what does he mean?*

A: He means there is no music of any kind to fill the silence on Earth.

Q: *What parts do Water Woman, Water Monster, and Cane-and-Conch play in this story?*

A: They are servants of Tezcatlipoca who help Quetzalcoatl build a bridge from Earth to the Sun.

Q: *What form does Quetzalcoatl take to reach the Sun?*

A: He takes the form of Wind.

Q: *When Quetzalcoatl reached the Sun, why did he not see any musicians wearing dark colors?*

A: There were no sad songs being played in the house of Sun.

Q: *Why did Sun order the musicians to be silent?*

A: He did not want the musicians to leave his world. He felt that if they stayed silent, Quetzalcoatl, in the form of Wind, would be unable to locate them.

Q: *What role does Tezcatlipoca take in making the musicians finally leave the house of Sun?*

A: He creates a powerful storm in the land of the Sun that makes the musicians want to leave.

Q: *Who learned to play music on Earth?*

A: Every living being, from humans to birds, but also non-living creations such as the ocean and the mountain streams.

EXPERT COMMENTARY

Was Quetzalcoatl real or imaginary? And just how special was he to the Aztecs?

Scholar Donna Rosenberg, wrote in her book, *World Mythology*, that experts on Aztec mythology think that the god Quetzalcoatl grew out of a combination of myth and fact. He was probably a real-life leader such as a priest or king who gave the Aztecs laws and rules to live by. It is known that a ruler of the Aztecs' ancestors, the Toltecs, took the name Quetzalcoatl in the tenth century.

Rosenberg adds,

> Scholars may argue whether Quetzalcoatl was one man or many, whether he was native to the Americas or a foreigner, whether he lived in one century or another. However, they all agree that his myth left a powerful, lasting impression on the major cultures of Central America.[1]

Quetzalcoatl's importance is reflected by his very special name, which derives from the radiantly beautiful quetzal bird. Inga Clendinnen is a scholar who has taught at several universities including Princeton University in New Jersey. She discusses the quetzal bird in her book, *Aztecs: An Interpretation*.

> All feathers were passionately valued [by the Aztecs], but the quetzal plume held a special place in the Mexica imagination. [Clendinnen uses the term "Mexica" to refer to the Aztec people, but not the entire Aztec empire.] It was rare, the shy male bird which grew the two long curving tail feathers living deep in the remote rain forests to the South. The feather filaments are light, long, and glossy, so that the smallest movement sets them shimmering. And the color, a gilded emerald haunted by a deep singing violet blue, is extraordinary: one of those visual experiences quite

impossible to bear in mind, so that each seeing is its own small miracle . . .

Few Mexica could have seen the majestic bannered flight of this extraordinary bird rippling across the sky, the trailing quetzal plumes sensitive to each shift and movement in the air, but even in stillness their import was clear . . . The Mexica called their most valued feathers and featherwork "the Shadows of the Sacred Ones," the marvelous projections into this dimmed world of the light, colour and exquisite delicacy of the world of the gods.[2]

8

THE BIRTH OF THE WAR GOD

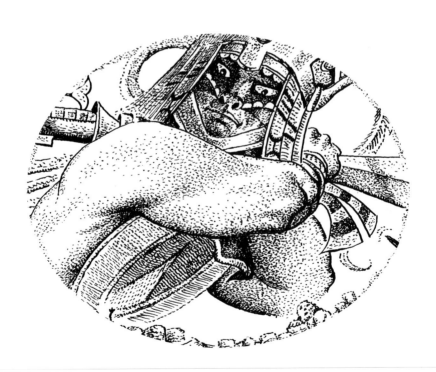

INTRODUCTION

Most cultures have cities or other places that are holy to them. The city of Jerusalem is holy to people of three different faiths, Jews, Christians, and Muslims. The Muslims' holiest cities are Mecca and Medina. Roman Catholics consider Vatican City, an independent state surrounded by Rome, Italy, a holy place. Even more recently established religions have their holy places. Members of the Mormon Church, which was founded in the United States in the nineteenth century, have their holiest shrines in Temple Square in Salt Lake City, Utah.

One of the Aztecs' holiest sites was a hill called Coatepec (Co-at-EH-pec). That mystical mountain was located near an ancient city known as Tollan, located about sixty miles northwest of present-day Mexico City. Every year, the Aztecs made a pilgrimage to Coatepec where they feasted in honor of their god Huitzilopochtli, whom they believed had been born on the hill.

Huitzilopochtli, who became the Aztecs' patron god, represented all the traits a soldier should have: He was courageous, in superb physical condition, and always victorious in battle. His name comes from two Aztec words: *huitzilin* which means "hummingbird," and *opochtli* which is the word for both "left" and "south." So the god's name probably meant "the hummingbird of the south."[1]

In addition to being the Aztecs' god of war, Huitzilopochtli was a shield and protector for his people. It was up to Huitzilopochtli to watch over and lead them to their place of destiny, or promised land. He assured his people that if they followed his directions, they would discover a place of unlimited sustenance where they would be a powerful nation. That place was to become the shining Aztec city of Tenochtitlan, which they built on an island in the middle of shimmering Lake Texcoco.

When the Aztec civilization was flourishing, the island city's population was about 250,000 people, equal to that of a medium-sized American city today. Visitors entered Tenochtitlan either by a dugout canoe or by foot across one of three extended causeways. The city proper was laid out in a series of canals and streets. The presence of the canals caused the Spanish invaders to refer to Tenochtitlan as "the Venice of the New World," because it reminded them of the historic city of Venice, Italy, which is also laced with canals.

In the center of Tenochtitlan was the main square. Aztec royalty lived in palaces surrounding the square, while commoners made their homes in small cottages on the outskirts of the city center. North of the square was the large Tlatelolco (t'la-tay-LOH-koh) market. Dominating the city skyline was the pyramid-shaped Great Temple. Only nobles were allowed to enter the temple.

While the north side of the Great Temple was dedicated to Tlaloc, the rain god, the southern side was dedicated to Huitzilopochtli. It was by the southern steps of the temple that the Aztecs' prisoners of war were placed over a sacrificial stone to have their hearts torn out. Their bodies were then tossed onto the base of the temple steps.

To the Aztecs, the main temple symbolized the magical mountain called Coatepec, the place where Huitzilopochtli was born.

THE BIRTH OF THE WAR GOD

Coatlicue (CO-at-lee-kway) was an honest woman who lived in the shadow of the mountain called Coatepec. Coatlicue had a daughter named Coyolxauhquil (koh-yohl-SHAU-wa-ki), an evil daughter named Malinalxochitl (mal-in-al-SHO-tch-it'l), and four hundred sons, collectively known as the Centzon Huitznahua (SENT-zon WEETS-na-wah). One day Coatlicue was working and performing religious rituals, in a ravine near Coatepec when she noticed a mysterious ball of feathers on the ground. She was fascinated by this odd, supernatural gift which seemed to have fallen from the heavens. Coatlicue felt a sudden an urge to keep the ball of feathers, so she picked it up and tucked it under her clothes. The feathers were held in place close to her body.

What Coatlicue did not realize was that the ball of feathers was magical and had impregnated her. Within months, her grown children noticed that their mother's belly was growing larger and larger. They insisted on knowing who the father was. When Coatlicue could not give them an answer, they became furious. They felt that their mother had dishonored their family, and should be punished by death.

Coatlicue was terrified, but she could feel the baby inside communicating with her. The baby was soothing her, telling her everything would be all right. When the time came to give birth, Coatlicue climbed to the top of Coatepec. Still enraged, her children followed her to the mountain summit with the intention of killing their mother.

However, just as they reached the top of Coatepec, the baby was born. He was named Huitzilopochtli. It was clear that he was no ordinary baby. Huitzilopochtli came into the world fully formed and clothed in armor, and holding a series of deadly weapons. He was ready to fight any enemy of his mother. His most dangerous weapon was a knife-like tool called a *xiuhcoatl* (shi-wuh-KO-atl), which means "fire serpent." Quickly, with the *xiuhcoatl*, he sliced off the oldest daughter's head and cut her body to pieces. Her remains fell down the mountainside to its base.

Huitzilopochtli then went on the attack against the Centzon Huitznahua. Even though these four hundred sons of his mother were his half-brothers, Huitzilopochtli recognized them as dangers. He killed several right away, then chased the others around the summit of Coatepec before killing several more. A few of his half-brothers escaped and survived, but Huitzilopochtli and Coatlicue were safe and healthy.

The Aztec people accepted Huitzilopochtli as their warrior god. In turn, he told them that he would lead them to a promised land, a place where they would live and prosper. He said, "Here I shall bring together the diverse peoples, and not in vain, for I shall conquer them, that I may see the house of jade, the house of gold, the house of quetzal feathers; the house of emeralds, the house of coral, the house of amethysts; the sundry feathers—the lovely cotinga feathers, the roseate spoonbill feathers, the trogon feathers—all the precious feathers; and the cacao of variegated colors, and the cotton of variegated colors! I shall see all this, for in truth it is my work, it was for this that I was sent here."[2]

One day, Huitzilopochtli was sleeping near his sister, Malinalxochitl. As she slept, Huitzilopochtli awoke and left to start his journey to lead the Aztec people to their new promised land. Malinalxochitl woke up and noticed her brother had left her. Her heart was filled with anger towards her brother. She led her followers to a mountain named Texcatepetl (TEKS-caat-eh-pet'l), where she gave birth to a son she called Copil (KOH-peel).

Meanwhile, Huitzilopochtli led the Aztec people to Coatepec, the mountain where he was born. The people believed this to be their promised land and settled there happily. But Huitzilopochtli decided it was not the right place. To force the people to give up their new homes at Coatepec, he punched a hole in a nearby dam which had been holding back a river. Once the hole was made, a torrent of water rushed over the land, killing the plants and animals that had been providing the Aztecs with food. So Huitzilopochtli led the people on another journey, this time to a place named Techcatitlan (tetch-kah-TEE-t'lan).

At Techcatitlan, Huitzilopochtli met his nephew, Copil, who had grown up to be even more evil than his mother. The uncle and nephew battled until Huitzilopochtli chased Copil to a place called Tepetzinco (teh-peh-T'ZIN-koo). Here, Huitzilopochtli captured and killed Copil, cutting off his head and tearing out his heart. Huitzilopochtli gave his nephew's heart to a servant and ordered him to throw it away in a forest of reeds.

Then, Huitzilopochtli went about his own business. For the next forty years, Huitzilopochtli and the Aztecs wandered through the wilderness looking for their special home. There were times when they thought they had found their promised land, but Huitzilopochtli was always looking out for his people. If they were in the wrong place, he made sure they moved on.

For example, one time they arrived and settled in a strange kingdom. Huitzilopochtli knew this was not their promised land. Under his power, the Aztecs killed the daughter of the king. They skinned the princess and had one of their priests wear her skin while they performed a ceremony. As soon as the king saw this brutal ritual, he forced the Aztecs to leave his land, just as Huitzilopochtli had planned. They continued on their long trek to find the special place they would call home.

At long last, their journey took the Aztecs to the shallow waters of Lake Texcoco. The people, carrying arrows and shields, crossed the lake and, as soon as they reached an island in the middle, one of the Aztec priests saw Huitzilopochtli in a vision. In this vision, the great god told the priest to watch for an eagle that would be sitting on a cactus called *tenochtli* (teh-NOTCH-t'li), or "stone cactus," while holding a snake in its beak. The cactus, Huitzilopochtli told the priest, had grown from the discarded heart of his wicked sister, Copil. The eagle was a physical embodiment of Huitzilopochtli.

The priest and his followers proceeded onward, in search of the vision. Then, next to some marsh grasses near a spring they caught sight of an eagle eating a serpent. It was sitting atop a cactus.

The story continues:

> And when the eagle saw the Mexicans, he bowed his head low . . . Its nest, its pallet, was of every kind of precious feather—of lovely coting feathers, roseate spoonbill feathers, quetzal feathers . . . And the god called out to them, he said to them, 'O Mexicans, it shall be there!'[3]

It was on that spot that the Aztecs founded what would become Tenochtitlan, their splendid home.

QUESTIONS AND ANSWERS

Q: *What was Coatlicue doing when she saw the mysterious ball of feathers?*

A: Coatlicue was working and performing religious rituals.

Q: *Why did Coatlicue's children feel she had dishonored their family?*

A: Coatlicue could not tell them who had fathered her baby.

Q: *What was Huitzilopochtli wearing when he was born, and how did it relate to his purpose as a god?*

A: Huitzilopochtli was born wearing armor. He was accepted as a warrior god and the protector of his people.

Q: *How did Huitzilopochtli let his people know that Coatepec was not their promised land?*

A: He made a hole in the nearby dam. The floodwaters killed the plants and animals that served to provide the Aztec people with food. This spurred them to move on, where they would find a promised land.

Q: *Why did the Aztecs kill the daughter of a king?*

A: They did it under the power of Huitzilopochtli. Upon learning of his daughter's murder, the king forced the Aztecs out of his kingdom. That was Huitzilopochtli's way of forcing his people to move on until they reached their promised land.

Q: *What image would let the Aztecs know they had reached their promised land?*

A: The Aztecs were searching for an eagle sitting on a cactus while the majestic bird held a snake in its beak.

EXPERT COMMENTARY

Experts interpret the birth and life of Huitzilopochtli in various ways. About a hundred years ago, a German scholar named Eduard Seler said that Huitzilopochtli represented the newly born sun shooting out burning rays. Seler went on to suggest that the Centzon Huitznahua, whom Huitzilopochtli conquered, represented the stars which submit to the sun at the dawn of each new day.

Historian Karl Taube points out that Huitzilopochtli's birth is also a symbol of the Aztecs' dominance over their neighbors. Taube says, "The birth of this god provided . . . the Aztecs' right to rule over their defeated enemies."[4]

Richard F. Townsend stresses in his book, *The Aztecs*, the importance of the birth and successes of Huitzilopochtli and how he was immortalized when they were constructing their home city in their promised land.

> At imperial Tenochtitlan centuries later, the Great Pyramid with Huitzilopochtli's shrine would be named Coatepetl, in commemoration of this mythic battle at the mountaintop, and at the pyramid's foot lay a huge dismembered sculpture of Coyolxauhqui.[5]

Another expert, Elizabeth Hill Boone, emphasizes how the Aztec people evolve over the course of the migration and become capable of building a civilization.

According to Boone:

> The Mexica migration story has all the elements of a transformational passage, whereby the Mexica are changed from their previous selves and are endowed with the characteristics necessary for their imperial success. They begin as . . . semi-barbarian people who exist by hunting, gathering, and occasionally employing agriculture, and emerge as suitable adversaries and allies to the powerful people in the valley.[6]

It is easy to note from this myth that many cultures have similar stories. For example, the birth of Huitzilopochtli was the result of an immaculate conception, just as the birth of Jesus, described in the New Testament of the Bible. As a fully formed god, Huitzilopochtli leads his people through forty years of wandering through the wilderness, the way Moses leads the Israelites for the same amount of time in the Old Testament of the Bible. In addition, the result of the forty years of searching in both the Aztec and Biblical stories was the arrival at their promised land.

 GLOSSARY

cactus—A spiny plant grown in deserts.

causeway—A raised roadway across water.

chimpana—A floating garden formed by piling up mud from a lake bottom.

civilization—A society of people, defined by their culture.

codice—A book written by the ancient Maya documenting their religious beliefs.

commoner—A person without a noble rank but not property of another person, like a slave.

conquistadors—Spanish conquerors who invaded the Mayan and Aztec lands in the 1500s.

Hueytecuihuitl—A major Aztec feast which lasted ten days.

macaw—A bird in the parrot family known for a long tail and colorful plumage.

maguey—A plant whose fibers were used to make paper used in codices and whose sap was used to make pulque.

maize—Corn.

milpa—A small garden plot cultivated by the ancient Maya.

nahual—The animal spirit form of a person as believed by the ancient Aztecs.

noble—A person of a high-ranking social class.

pohatok—A ball game played by the ancient Maya, most similar to basketball than any other major sport.

professor—Title for an experienced college or university teacher.

pulque—An alcoholic beverage made from the fermented sap of the maguey.

quetzal—A bird known for its brilliantly colored feathers.

sacrifice—The killing of a human being or other animal done to please one's god.

temple—A building used as a place of worship.

tlachtli—A ball game played by the ancient Aztec, resembling a combination of basketball and soccer.

ulli—The small rubber ball used by the Maya to play pohatok.

ᗒᗩ Chapter Notes ᗒᗩ

Preface

1. Editors of Time-Life Books, *Aztecs: Reign of Blood & Splendor*, (Alexandria, Va: Time-Life Books, 1992), p. 48.

Chapter 1. The Creation of People According to the Popol Vuh

1. Dennis Tedlock, translator, *Popol Vuh: The Mayan Book of the Dawn of Life*, (New York: Touchstone Books, 1986), p. 23.

2. Ibid., pp. 31–32.

3. Donna Rosenberg, *World Mythology: An Anthology of the Great Myths and Epics* (Lincolnwood, Ill.: Passport Books, 1986), p. 470.

4. Roberta H. Markman and Peter T. Markman, *The Flayed God: The Mythology of Mesoamerica* (New York: HarperCollins Publishers, 1992), p. 108.

5. Rosenberg, p. 471.

6 "Mayan Writing" <www.execpc.com/~urbanlee/MayaWrit.html> (June 28, 1999).

7. Markman, p. 105.

8. Ibid.

9. Ralph Nelson, *Popol Vuh* (Boston: Houghton Mifflin Company, 1976), p. 13.

Chapter 2. Seven Macaw and His Sons

1. David Friedel, Linda Schele and Joy Parker, *Maya Cosmos: Three Thousand Years on the Shaman's Path*, (New York: William Morrow and Co., Inc., 1993), p. 211.

2. Ibid., p. 213.

3. Ibid.

Chapter 3. The Origin of the Sun and the Moon

1. Linda Schele and Peter Mathews, *The Code of Kings: The Language of Seven Sacred Maya Temples and Tombs* (New York: Scribner, 1998) p. 213.

Chapter 4. The Hero Twins

1. Donald Tedlock, translator, *Popol Vuh: The Mayan Book of the Dawn of Life*, (New York: Touchstone Books, 1986), p. 144.

2. Timothy R. Roberts, *Myths of the World: Gods of the Maya, Aztecs, and Incas* (New York: Metro Books, 1996), p. 36.

3. Linda Schele and David Freidel, *A Forest of Kings: The Untold Story of the Ancient Maya* (New York: William Morrow and Co., 1990) p. 76.

4. David Friedel, *Linda Schele and Joy Parker, Maya Cosmos: Three Thousand Years on the Shaman's Path*, (New York: William Morrow and Co., Inc., 1993), p. 349.

5. Michael D. Coe, *The Maya* (New York: Thames and Hudson, 1999), p. 202.

Chapter 5. The Creation of the World

1. Veronica Ions, *The World's Mythology in Colour* (New York: Hamlyn Publishing Group Limited, 1974), p. 248.

2. Ibid.

3. Ibid.

4. Elizabeth Hill Boone, *The Aztec World* (Washington, D.C.: Smithsonian Books, 1994), p. 98.

Chapter 6. Feeding the Aztec People

1. Jane Brody, *Jane Brody's Good Food Book* (New York: W.W. Norton & Co., 1985), p. 49.

2. *Encyclopedia of World Religions: Judaism, Christianity, Islam, Buddhism, Zen, Hinduism, Prehistoric & Primitive Religions* (London, England: Octopus Books Limited, 1975), p. 52.

3. Richard F. Townsend, *The Aztecs* (New York: Thames and Hudson, 1992), p. 115.

4. *Encyclopedia of World Religions: Judaism, Christianity, Islam, Buddhism, Zen, Hinduism, Prehistoric & Primitive Religions*, p. 52.

Chapter 7. The Creation of Music

1. Donna Rosenberg, *World Mythology: An Anthology of the Great Myths and Epics* (Lincolnwood, Ill.: Passport Books, 1986), p. 483

2. Inga Clendinnen, *Aztecs: An Interpretation* (New York: Cambridge University Press, 1991), pp. 217–218.

Chapter 8. The Birth of the War God

1. Nigel Davies, *The Aztecs* (Norman, Okla.: University of Oklahoma Press, 1973), pp. 17–18.

2. Thelma D. Sullivan, as quoted in Roberta H. Markman and Peter T. Markman, *The Flayed God: The Mythology of Mesoamerica* (New York: HarperCollins Publishers, 1992), pp. .396–397.

3. Ibid., p. 408.

4. Karl Taube, *Aztec and Maya Myths* (Austin, Tex: University of Texas Press, 1993), pp. 47, 49.

5. Richard F. Townsend, *The Aztecs* (New York: Thames and Hudson, 1992), p. 60.

6. Elizabeth Hill Boone, *The Aztec World* (Washington, D.C.: Smithsonian Books, 1994), pp. 36–37.

▷◁FURTHER READING▷◁

Arnold, Caroline. *City of the Gods: Mexico's Ancient City of Teotihuacan*. New York: Clarion Books, 1994.

Fisher, Leonard Everett. *Gods and Goddesses of the Ancient Maya*. New York: Holiday House, Inc., 1999.

Galvin, Irene Flum. *Cultures of the Past: The Ancient Maya*. Tarrytown, N.Y.: Benchmark Books, 1997.

Gerson, Mary Jo. *People of the Corn: A Mayan Story*. Boston: Little, Brown and Company, 1995.

Greger, C. Shana. *The Fifth and Final Sun: An Ancient Aztec Myth of the Sun's Origin*. Boston: Houghton Mifflin, 1994.

Lattimore, Deborah Nourse. *Why There is No Arguing in Heaven: A Mayan Myth*. New York: Harper & Row Publishers, 1989.

Matthews, Sally Schofer. *The Sad Night: The Story of an Aztec Victory and a Spanish Loss*. New York: Clarion Books, 1994.

McDermott, Gerald. *Musicians of the Sun*. New York, Simon & Schuster, 1997.

Meyer, Carolyn and Gallenkamp, Charles. *The Mystery of the Ancient Maya*. New York: Margaret K. McElderry Books, 1995.

Montejo, Victor. *Popol Vuh: A Sacred Book of the Maya*. Toronto: Groundwood Books, 1999.

Pyramid of the Sun—Pyramid of the Moon. New York: Macmillan Publishing Company, 1988.

INTERNET ADDRESSES

Arte Maya Tz'utuhil art gallery (modern Maya paintings and other works of art)
<http://www.artemaya.com>

Aztec Civilization for Children
<http://home.freeuk.net/elloughton13/aztecs.htm>

Ancient Aztecs
<http://library.thinkquest.org/27981/>

Popol Vuh—A Creation Story
<http://www.jaguarpaw.com/Popol.html>

◁ INDEX ▷